JB JOSSEY-BASS™
A Wiley Brand

Nonprofit Website Essentials

124 Tips, Techniques and Ideas to Add Value to Your Website

Scott C. Stevenson, Editor

WILEY

Nonprofit Website Essentials
124 Tips, Techniques and Ideas
To Add Value to Your Website

Published by

Stevenson, Inc.

P.O. Box 4528 • Sioux City, Iowa • 51104

Phone 712.239.3010 • Fax 712.239.2166

www.stevensoninc.com

Nonprofit Website Essentials
124 Tips, Techniques and Ideas to Add Value to Your Website

TABLE OF CONTENTS

Nonprofit Website Essentials

124 Tips, Techniques and Ideas to Add Value to Your Website

TABLE OF CONTENTS

Nonprofit Website Essentials

124 Tips, Techniques and Ideas to Add Value to Your Website

 ## 1 Share Message in Virtual World

For a creative way to connect with donors, volunteers and others, create an online world related to your cause.

Members of the Colorado Association of Libraries (CAL), Lakewood, CO, can join an interest group based on the virtual world of Second Life from Linden Lab (San Francisco, CA), an online 3-D interactive virtual reality program that allows users to socialize and participate in individual and group activities.

CAL has paid for the land rental and custom building design in the virtual online world, offering free participation to all members. Second Life hosts continuing education classes on how to develop personal avatars and has already hosted several meetings and programs in-world.

The organization is also establishing a presence on Second Life through a virtual library, virtual workshops, conferences and links to websites where members learn more about smart environmental choices.

"The library is not necessarily a place anymore, but an access to information, especially in remote areas," says Jody Howard, association president. "Second Life helps connect members with common interests. It's just another way to use relevant technology to bring people together."

Source: Jody K. Howard, President, Colorado Association of Libraries, Thornton, CO. Phone (303) 859-1242.
E-mail: jodyhoward@comcast.net

 ## 2 Entice Visitors With a Customizable Webpage

Customizing your website to suit varied visitors will set your organization apart. It allows for visitors to be exposed to the most pertinent information while giving your organization a chance to customize the news you share.

"We are always looking for new ways to engage our users and to give them the information they are looking for faster and more efficiently. It also allows us to provide unique event banners and to display them to the appropriate groups," says Rick Stutz, coordinator of e-communications, Juniata College (Huntington, PA). "By selecting the type of user you are, we are able to customize news, events and suggested links to make your experience on our website more fulfilling and informative."

In order to provide users with a more personal experience, Stutz says, they give visitors five categories to choose from as they enter the site: campus community, prospective students, current students, parents and alumni. This customization gives users easy access to all relevant information as soon as they enter the site.

A customization feature is especially helpful for those users

---

Customize Your Webpage

Would a customizable webpage might bring benefits to your organization? Here are five steps to making it operational:

1. Determine your budget.
2. Determine which areas you would like to customize.
3. Make sure you system is capable of handling the updates.
4. Meet with IT staff or an outside source to discuss your plan of action.
5. Implement your new customized webpage.

Content not available in this edition

A screenshot of Juniata College's customizable webpage. Users can select from five categories to customize the page.

who are not adept at website navigation. It takes the guesswork out of finding information by eliminating lengthy searches. Visitors will also appreciate the option of viewing your site in a way that reflects their relationship with your organization. "So far this tool has been met with much success, but we are always testing how to provide the best experience for our varied users," says Stutz.

If your organization is interested in customizing your site, speak to your Web designer or IT staff regarding the specifics. "Nearly all of our website features are created in-house with the team effort of both marketing and IT. Though not simple, it was one of the easier features of our new site to create and implement," says Stutz. He estimates the cost to develop the organization's customizable Web page in-house was about $10,000.

Source: Rick Stutz, Coordinator of E-Communications, Juniata College, Huntingdon, PA. Phone (814) 883-6580.
E-mail: stutzr@juniata.edu. Website: http://www.juniata.edu

Make Your Website Accessible to Those With Disabilities

For any organization, having a website provides an avenue to market your services and provide members with news and other updates. It is important to reach as many people as possible and designing a website that is handicap accessible will allow you to reach a more diverse group of people.

In 2001, the Perkins School for the Blind (Watertown, MA) decided to redesign its website to make it accessible for visitors with disabilities. "To quote one of our Accessibility Committee members, 'We felt it was critical to create a site where everyone benefits from access to the same information — where everyone was equal,'" says Kimberly Kittredge, webmaster.

The school knows how important it is to provide visitors with all the tools they need to learn about the organization and navigate the site easily. Every nonprofit would benefit from making their site more accessible. "Not only is it important for Perkins and other organizations to make information accessible for the user, it's also in every organization's best interest to be accessible. Increased accessibility leads to increased usability," she says.

Kittredge says WAI-compliant sites tend to rate better with search engine optimization, which will increase the overall visibility of your website. WAI, or Web Accessibility Initiative, is a set of guidelines that specify what a website must include to be accessible to people with disabilities.

Making your site accessible to a wider audience will take time. Reach out to the community and find out which features might be most helpful to those who visit your site. It might also be worthwhile to speak with other organizations that have already been through this process to get advice. Kittredge says, "When we set out to redesign the site, we created our own Accessibility Committee comprising of Perkins staff, outside professionals and alumni who are blind, have low vision or are sighted to help guide and review the design and programming process."

Source: Kimberly Emrick Kittredge, Webmaster, Perkins School for the Blind, Watertown, MA. Phone (617) 972-7350. E-mail: Kimberly.Kittredge@perkins.org. Website: www.perkins.org

---

 Drive Visitors to Your Website

Drive traffic to your website by creating and maintaining a user-friendly and informative site.

Elizabeth Thomason, director of communications, Saint Edward's School (Vero Beach, FL), shares some website design tips:

- Keep information current.
- Write succinctly. Copy should be brief, easy to read.
- Format pages no larger than 1024 X 768 pixels.
- Convert what's already in print to a PDF and have it available for download.
- Be sensitive when identifying minors or people without their permission.
- Have tons of photos (format them at 72 dpi).
- Place your organization's contact information or mission statement on an obvious page.
- Choose colors that reflect your institution but are soothing to the eye. Remember, less is more.
- Proof copy with several sets of eyes.
- Make sure the navigation is intuitive and try not to bury useful information too deep.
- Involve a Web committee to increase buy-in and ensure information accurately reflects your institution.

Source: Elizabeth Thomason, Director of Communications, Saint Edward's School, Vero Beach, FL. Phone (772) 492-2351. E-mail: ethomason@steds.org

 Global Reach of Media

In the age where most media outlets have a website, new considerations arise when communicating with local media.

A media relations strategy tailored to the global reach of Web-based content is essential. The key is to remember that once something is conveyed to the media, it is most likely going to turn up in search engine results about your organization. This means every statement you make to the media has the potential to reach a global audience.

Depending on the situation you may choose to withhold information you otherwise would share simply to avoid spreading the word beyond a comfortable region. However, remember what may seem like reason for caution can also work to your advantage in certain situations. When you are specifically trying to appeal to a large audience, for a fundraising effort perhaps, the speedy spread of information across the Internet will most likely work in your favor. In cases like this it's nice to know a small article published in your town newspaper has the potential to reach a number of readers far greater than the population of the paper's delivery area.

Web-based Press Releases Present More Options

Web-based releases have several advantages over traditional printed press releases. For starters, they can be e-mailed to media contacts, placed on your organization's website, easily changed or updated and may include maps, links and other graphics.

"In print format, releases often include attachments such as a fact sheet, photo of the president, the president's biography, a map showing where the company is located, etc.," says Wilma Mathews, director of constituent relations, Arizona State University (ASU) in Tempe, AZ. "In a Web-based release, you can still have all these elements, just in an easier presentation and with options on how to include additional information."

Web-based releases allow you to include links to other pertinent information without having to create a lengthy release, saving readers time and allowing them the option of following the links to gain further information.

"You can use hyperlinks within the body of the news release that will take the reader directly to the president's biography or a photo or map," says Mathews. "The challenge is not to overdo it. Don't load up a news release with hyperlinks." ASU's Web-based news releases often include links to research papers, other published articles or websites.

If your organization has yet to produce Web-based releases, or if you are looking to pump up their impact, look for examples from other local organizations to obtain layout ideas. Also consider checking with local media outlets for guidelines regarding Web-based releases. Some outlets may prefer e-mailed releases over printed ones.

"For media who prefer using Web-based releases, communicating with them is faster and perhaps easier," says Mathews. "And Web-based releases — like all Web-based sites and items — are easier to update and share" than mailed or faxed pieces.

Creating Web-based releases may take an initial time investment, but once you have a system for creating and updating releases, the process will become simpler, she says. "The process is streamlined if you have all support files (e.g., biographies, fact sheets, photos, maps, etc.) online and up to date.

> *'The challenge is not to overdo it. Don't load up a news release with hyperlinks.'*

Writing a Web-based release shouldn't take any more time than writing a traditional release. Setting up links takes time because you must check to make sure the links are correct and the linked-to information is current."

Mathews details some of the ways you can track the effectiveness of a Web-based release, saying: "A Web-based release will only make a big impact with either a media contact or a reader if the content is relevant, current, reliable or useful to either one or both. You'll know it was a hit with the media contact if s/he uses it in some other format: blog, newspaper, news items, etc. You'll know a reader thought it was a hit if you insert some kind of cookie or other tracking device that will show you where the reader went after reading the release — to a hyperlink, URL, comment page, etc."

Source: Wilma Mathews, Director of Constituent Relations, Arizona State University, Tempe, AZ. Phone (480) 727-6031. E-mail: wkm23@asu.edu

 ## Technology Boosts Involvement of Young Alums

Engaging young people in your cause can help them to become lifelong supporters. One way to do so is to connect with them in a way they understand — online.

Carrie Moore, assistant director, donor relations, Texas Christian University (TCU) of Fort Worth, TX, says keeping young alums involved has been a struggle. But by using viral marketing through websites like Facebook (www.facebook.com), she says, they are noticing an increase in the number of young alums starting to attend annual events.

Currently, TCU has 2,664 friends on its Facebook alumni site.

In another way that helps young alums to stay easily and quickly connected, TCU staff created Froglinks.com,

an online community named after the university's mascot, the Horned Frog. This site allows alums to read and leave class notes about their career changes, marriages and growing families; post classified ads; learn about upcoming events; find fellow alums through an online directory and get career placement help.

Moore says her experience in trying to engage young alums has left her with one bit of advice. "Get involved in all the technology you can and start now!"

Source: Carrie Moore, Assistant Director, Donor Relations, Texas Christian University, Fort Worth, TX. Phone (817) 257-6965. E-mail: cmoore2@tcu.edu

Guestbook Provides Outlet for Questions, Connections

An online guestbook offers a forum for persons to let their voices be heard and a resource of valuable feedback for your organization.

"The main purpose of our guestbook is to give our website visitors, as well as our worldwide ACU community, a place to touch base, ask questions or stay in touch," says Carmen Foster, director of Web communication, university relations, AbileneChristian University (ACU) of Abilene, TX. "With all the new Web 2.0 communities available today, it amazes me how many people still use and view our guestbook."

ACU has featured an online guestbook for more than eight years. The idea came from the director of Web integration and programming, who also wrote the original program.

"The guestbook is one of those tools that has been around a long time, but still has its place," Foster says. "I find it to be the preferred method for those visitors who want to find you and ask a question or make a comment without the threat of mass marketing being pushed at them. If they leave an e-mail address, we respond to their question or concern. They don't have to create an account or log in to leave a comment."

Typical reasons people use the guestbook, she says, include leaving testimonials, questions or comments. Prospective students communicate an interest in ACU or ask for information; alumni are sometimes looking to reconnect with friends.

When creating an online guestbook it is important to designate staff members to review the entries and respond to or approve comments as necessary, she says: "I am the one who administrates/reviews the guestbook entries. I am notified by e-mail every time there is a submission. If I do not know the answer, I forward it to someone who can help them.

"Our programmers have written a Web interface where I can view the entries and approve them for display on our website. We get eight to 10 legitimate entries a week, and roughly half of those require a response. I delete all entries that list a link to a business or try to sell you something.

"Our guestbook Web pages were viewed roughly 99,858 times in 2007," Foster says.

An online guestbook allows your organization to share information and keep in touch with valued community members, Foster adds: "The guestbook has been a good way to interact with the entire ACU community, regardless of age or location, and give them a place to tell their version of the ACU story. When you look at how many people are interacting with us through our guestbooks, you can see it is still a valuable communications tool, especially for those who are hesitant to create an account in an online community."

Creating an Online Guestbook

Online guestbooks can be especially helpful at connecting community members during a time of crisis or grief, says Carmen Foster, director of Web communications, university relations, Abilene Christian University (ACU) of Abilene, TX.

"The times that have been the most active (for ACU's online guestbook) are when the ACU community is in a state of highly emotional bonding, such as the memorials posted when we grieved the loss of a student, professor or long-time president, John C. Stevens," Foster says.

"Those of us in the university relations division knew that Dr. John Stevens was a beloved president and that many alumni, faculty, staff and students would like to share their memories. Ron Hadfield, our assistant VP for university communication, suggested we honor him with a website called Remembering John Christopher Stevens. We felt that a special guestbook would be a good way to allow the entire ACU community to tell the story. And 60 people in a 15-day period did just that."

Content not available in this edition

Source: Carmen M. Foster, Director of Web Communication, University Relations, Abilene Christian University, Abilene, TX. Phone (325) 674-4932. E-mail: carmen.foster@acu.edu

Simplify Website Navigation

Don't let the enormous amount of information on your website deter visitors from browsing. Consider using a site map and search feature combination on your site to make navigation easier.

A site map is a single page that contains links to all of the pages on your site. Another way to help users find information quickly is to allow them to enter what they are seeking into a search feature. Being able to search for a specific event or category will be beneficial to visitors who are less familiar with navigating the Web.

 Place a Staff Listing On Your Website

Consider placing a detailed staff listing on your organization's website. It will serve as a great resource for the community.

You can include detailed information (e.g., e-mail addresses, number of years with the organization and photos) or just a general department listing with one main contact phone number and e-mail address. Make sure the staff listing is divided by department or alphabetically for easy access.

 Include Historical Info in Online Media Kit

Including an extensive online media kit on your website will be a valuable resource for media contacts and staff members alike. Incorporating information about the history of your organization will further educate those researching your organization.

Sharing media-related information online also allows your organization to update and modify information quickly when the need arises without having to reprint traditional press kit materials.

Staff at Rollins College (Winter Park, FL) created an online media kit five years ago when they were expanding media resources on the college's website, says Ann Marie Varga, assistant vice president, office of public relations and communications. The online resource took several days to create and is updated annually.

The kit includes information on historic buildings and events, a link to a frequently asked questions section and other information. In 2007, staff updated the Rollins News Center with media tip sheets, an expert resource guide, the media kit and more. This year they added a section with faculty editorials.

The most important elements for an online media kit, she says, are historical in nature: founding; motto; traditions; and information on landmark buildings, significant events and points of pride.

Even with an online media database, Varga notes that most media contacts still want to talk to the communications staff directly, so be sure to include how to reach key people for firsthand information.

Source: Ann Marie Varga, Assistant Vice President, Office of Public Relations & Communications, Rollins College, Winter Park, FL. Phone (407) 646-2159. Website: www.rollins.edu/news/

 Make Your Website Press Friendly

How well does your website do in terms of connecting news media with key information and personnel in an easy-to-navigate manner?

Website design and maneuverability are crucial to nonprofits seeking positive publicity. Make information hard to find, and a reporter or editor may just go on to the next organization for the information he or she seeks.

"When your PR department is home asleep, your website is your only representative to the press," says Mark Shapiro, principal, Davis Marrin Communications (San Diego, CA).

With this in mind, take a close look at your website and revamp it where needed to garner the easiest access to important information and persons.

Shapiro shares the following tips that he says will keep the press happy and make them want to return to your website:

1. **Don't hide the contact info.** Make sure the press contacts are obvious. List them on the news page, on the contact us page and on each press release.

2. **Make links to a real person's e-mail address,** not to a general mailbox where you just type in your inquiry and only hope that someone will know where to forward the inquiry in a timely manner.

3. **Make sure your site information is up-to-date.** Journalists may take information directly from your site without contacting you to check facts first. Check often to make sure outdated information is removed and current information is given prominent play.

4. **Make your press release section searchable by date and topic.**

5. **Make sure all media inquiries are followed up quickly.** "Many important editors contact you when they need information immediately — not tomorrow."

Source: Mark Shapiro, Manager and Principal, Davis Marrin Communications, San Diego, CA. Phone (858) 573-0736. E-mail: mshapiro@davismarrin.com

13 Create Online Photo Database

Storing your organization's photos online and allowing easy access to the audiences allow you to share new images quickly while reducing the number of time-consuming photo requests you receive.

Staff with Central Washington University (CWU) of Ellensburg, WA, created the PhotoHunter online archival photo website in spring 2007, says Becky L. Watson, director, public relations and marketing.

"PhotoHunter can be used by any faculty, staff or student to view and download CWU photos," Watson says. "My entire staff helped develop the idea into the type of site we thought the university needed. We then got the administration's buy-in."

Watson and her staff sent a request for proposal to CWU information technology students, who take on such projects for course credit. Four students accepted the project and worked to successfully produce the interactive website.

The site is managed by one of the university photographers with occasional reviews from Watson, who notes that the university's existing server offered ample storage for the 800-some photos.

"The upkeep is minimal, and includes changing out photos periodically and reviewing for appropriate tags," she says. "We put so much thought into the categories when we created the site that we've had to do very little updating."

Photos are organized into nine categories: architecture, indoors, outdoors, portraits, president, sports, staff, students and teaching/learning. All photos were taken by university photographers. There is no cost to students, faculty or staff to access the site, and the images can be used for any university publication or website.

To publicize the launch, Watson and her staff created an on-campus campaign that included a notice in the university bulletin, e-mail blast and announcement on the university's Intranet.

Yearly reminder e-mails keep faculty, staff and students aware of the site.

For nonprofits considering such an online resource, Watson recommends coordinating with your IT department; getting buy-in from the organization's leaders; keeping the site simple to use and thanking everyone involved in the project.

Source: Becky L. Watson, Director, Public Relations and Marketing, Central Washington University, Ellensburg, WA. Phone (509) 963-1117.

 14 Promote Your Stories On Others' Websites

Seek out ways to get your news stories on websites other than your own.

"I promote use of our stories and press releases on the websites of affiliated organizations," says Aubrey Streit, director of communications, Bethany College (Lindsborg, KS). "For example, we recently wrote and distributed a press release about a service learning trip our students took to help with recovery efforts in Greensburg, KS. We received coverage on several key sites, including the National Association of Intercollegiate Athletics and Central States Synod of the Evangelical Lutheran Church in America (ELCA)."

Streit targets organizations that have a link to the school. "The Central States Synod of the ELCA is one of the synods that support our school, so the readers of their site may already have an interest in Bethany College," she says.

She also recommends listening to people in and around your organization regarding websites they frequently read.

To streamline the process of reaching out to websites beyond those of media contacts, Streit and her staff added e-mail addresses for other appropriate websites to their media distribution list to make it easy to e-mail them relevant news releases.

"What we gain from story placements on the Web are wider exposure on the Internet, as well as exposure to targeted audiences of readers. These readers get referred back to our Web page," says Streit.

"Because Web links are easy to communicate, we routinely share press coverage in our on-campus e-mail newsletter," she says. "This helps people on campus realize that the stories they contribute to do matter and get read, and helps them take pride in Bethany."

In addition, she says, sending stories to nonprofits affiliated with the college's mission has strengthened relationships with those important organizations.

Pitching your stories to other organizations is no different than pitching to media contacts, Streit says. "Know the website, have an idea of who its readers are, and be able to connect your story to the site's purpose and readers."

Source: Aubrey Streit, Director of Communications, Bethany College, Lindsborg, KS. Phone (785) 227-3380, ext. 8274. E-mail: streita@bethanylb.edu

Manage Mass E-mailing With Precision

Managing a massive distribution list can be an exhausting task because keeping your list organized and updated to accommodate mass e-mailing takes immense energy and forethought.

"Buy a product to handle mass e-mail for you. There are many on the market now, some even specialize in particular niches, like universities," says Melissa Reichley, director of development communications, American University (Washington, DC).

American University began using an e-mail marketing service (www.bronto.com) in 2005. Reichley says, "We were impressed with the product's features, such as the ability to pre-schedule messages, message tracking, automatic formatting of HTML or text e-mail for the recipient and the ability for users to unsubscribe themselves and manage other preferences." Using an e-mail marketing product enables you to streamline the time and energy involved by giving you and your recipients access to such features.

Since implementing the e-mail marketing service, Reichley says, "We have sent hundreds of messages to thousands of alumni and donors announcing events and news, distributing e-newsletters and sending pledge reminders on a weekly, if not daily, basis. Now that we're comfortable using Bronto, we plan to take it to the next level by refining our alumni tracking and

marketing efforts."

Consider your organization's members when weighing e-mail distribution options. "The one caveat I'd make about mass e-mail is that those who are in front of their computers daily tend to forget sometimes that we have constituents who don't use a computer regularly. I'm a huge fan of mass e-mail, but I also believe there's still room for targeted mailing and using e-mail for follow up or pre-mail," Reichley says.

Source: Melissa Reichley, Director of Development Communications, American University, Washington, DC. Phone (202) 885-5930. E-mail: mreich@american.edu

Don't Lose Track of Your E-mail Subscriptions

You're most likely familiar with e-mail distribution lists because you use them to quickly get your message heard by many contacts at once. Remember, managing your subscriptions to others' distribution lists can be a similarly effective communications practice.

While signing up for newsletters online, keep good record of the newsletters' sources. Make a list of the distribution lists you have signed up for so you know from whom to expect correspondence. This will also enable you to protect these messages from ending up in your spam folder. It will make filtering through unwanted messages easier. Managing your subscriptions helps you complete a clear picture of your entire communications effort, outbound and inbound. Knowing which organizations are contacting you regularly can be as valuable as knowing your own distribution lists.

 ### Increase Online Involvement

To increase online visits from your nonprofit's important constituents — customers, donors, the media and others — make your website involvement rich by adding features such as:

✓ Members-only interactive groups.

✓ Online surveys.

✓ Online threaded discussion groups.

✓ Online chat groups or bulletin boards.

✓ Chat sessions with experts.

✓ Online book clubs, alumni groups and other affinity groups related to and appropriate for your cause.

 ### Match Domain Name With Organization Name

Having a website domain name that matches your organization's name makes it easier for visitors to find your site.

If your site name has nothing to do with your organization, it will not only be difficult to find in a search, but people will be less likely to take notice of it. Having a domain name that is the same as your organization's name will attract potential donors and volunteers to your site with ease. It will also help solidify name recognition within the community.

Obtaining your domain name is easy. Sites such as www.networksolutions.com/whois/ allow you to search domain names to see if yours is available. Keep in mind that an accurate domain name will help carve out your place on the Web.

Consider Creating a Blog to Encourage Interactive Communication

Many organizations are creating their own blogs to share information with their community and encourage a dialogue about issues facing their industry.

The communications office at Middlebury College (Middlebury, VT) maintains three blogs: a news blog; a president's blog and a dean's blog.

Free Software Creates Blogs

Tim Etchells, director, interactive communications, says the blogs are maintained completely in-house, and were created at no cost. For the news blog, they used the Blogger platform (www.blogger.com/start). For the president's and dean's blogs, they used WordPress (http://wordpress.org).

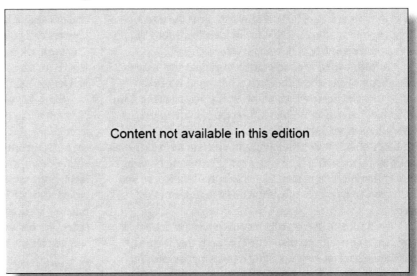

Content not available in this edition

Etchells says one benefit of blogs is how they provide two-way communication with community members in a way not previously possible.

While each blog has a comments feature that allows community members to share their thoughts on the information being posted, not every post receives comments. On average, the president's posts can receive three to 10 comments per posting. The news blog, which lists news coverage, provides Middlebury staff with a place to share outside news stories with alumni and other community members.

Blog Platforms Available for All Levels of Expertise

Etchells says that while his staff used free software and in-house technical know-how to develop and host blogs, a variety of websites will host online blogs for a monthly or yearly fee. Organizations without the technical knowledge or ability to host a weblog, might consider one of these externally hosted blogs. One such service, TypePad (www.typepad.com), offers subscriptions from $107.40 to $1,079.40 per year.

Regardless of which platform you choose, Etchells says, organizations needn't fear the process of creating and maintaining a blog. "The process is a simple one. You don't need to be an expert, you can learn as you go."

The more frequently you post new information, the more likely you are to generate traffic. Etchells recommends updating blogs at least weekly to hold interest. To further generate traffic, he says, make sure to publicize blogs. In addition to linking to Middlebury's website, these blogs are mentioned in e-mails to alumni and parents.

Statistics Illustrate Blog Traffic

Etchells shares statistics regarding traffic received by two of Middlebury's blogs:

- In its first eight months, the dean's blog (http://blogs.middlebury.edu/onedeans-view) was hosted by wordpress and (http://deanofthecollege.wordpress.com) averaged 1,300 visits a month, with a high of more than 2,000 and a low of 1,100.

- The president's blog (http://blogs.middlebury.edu/rononmiddlebury) was hosted by wordpress and (http://rononmiddlebury.wordpress.com) averaged 2,000 hits a month, with a monthly high of 4,000 and a low of 1,000.

Source: Tim Etchells, Director, Interactive Communications, Middlebury College, Middlebury, VT. Phone (802) 443-5707. Website: www.middlebury.edu

Check Out Online Blogs

Numerous colleges and other organizations throughout the country are now hosting blogs, many of which are written by students and faculty members themselves.

Here is a list of a few of the colleges with online logs:

❏ **http://blogs.ucollege.edu/**
— Various blogs maintained by both students and faculty members.

❏ **http://blogs.goucher.edu/**
— A faculty blog as well as a blog focusing on the class of 2010.

❏ **http://blogs.scb.rit.edu/**
— Multiple faculty and staff blogs.

❏ **http://www.talklyon.com/**
— A blog which focuses on many aspects of campus life, written by students.

Flash E-mails Invigorate Correspondence

Flash e-mails are a sophisticated way to grab the attention of those on your mailing list and retain their focus long enough to deliver a complete and solid message.

"A flash e-mail is an interactive webpage that uses the technology of Macromedia Flash. The e-mail is usually linked to a webpage, which allows readers to view the flash video file," says Bob Williams, director of communications, Asheville School (Asheville, NC). "Flash allows users to see fancy slideshows, animation and video in a small format that's easily viewable on a Web page. The beauty of using flash is that most computers have flash pre-installed, so you don't have to worry about compatibility issues for other users."

Use flash e-mails to make announcements or introduce new campaigns with cutting-edge eye candy that is sure to make an impact on viewers. Flash e-mails can be used for various occasions, from event invitations to simply sharing a holiday wish. "The idea was prompted two years ago when one of our alums forwarded us a flash e-mail from Princeton University that included a song from the university's choir. The feedback has been outstanding," says Williams. "These flash e-mails really bring back great memories for our alumni and let our alumni know we're embracing new technology."

How do you design flash e-mails for your organization? "My advice to other organizations is to do research before attempting to create these kinds of e-mails," Williams says. "Sometimes all it takes to start your flash e-mail is sitting down with a Web developer who understands the technology. Start with a simple idea before trying anything too complicated. Try to limit your videos to less than three minutes and keep the message positive. If you plan to redesign your website, talk to your webmaster about adding a simple content manager feature for your video files."

Source: Bob Williams, Director of Communications, Asheville School, Asheville, NC. Phone (828) 254-6345 ext. 4042. E-mail: williamsb@ashevilleschool.org

---

 ### Website Marketing 101

Make sure each page of your website has an easy-to-find link back to your home page.

Also, are your website pages intended to make a call to action? Is the hoped-for action clear to visitors? If not, redesign the page to make it obvious what you'd like visitors to do.

 ### Craft Effective Subject Lines

If you want the media to open your e-mail news release, stay away from generic subject lines like *press release* or *for immediate release*. While you should not mislead readers with overhyped subject lines, you do want to attract interest. Find a hook, a way to capture your reader's attention, but keep it believable, truthful and concise. Avoid using the release's headline in the subject line.

 ### Increase the Value of Your E-mail Signature

E-mail may be one of the most powerful, yet subtle, marketing tools available. If you're only including your contact information in your signature file, you're missing a simple and cost-effective way to promote the work your organization is doing.

Consider the following suggestions to add value to your e-mail signature:

- **Promote an upcoming event or activity.** Include a link to your website where people can purchase tickets or get information online.

- **Support your annual appeal.** Include a link to your website where people can donate securely online.

- **Cross-promote with a partner organization.** Work with an organization that serves a similar population and provide links to each other's websites (e.g.; the Make-A-Wish Foundation might provide a link to the Leukemia & Lymphoma Society and vice versa). Make sure each organization's constituents can benefit from the services provided by the other organization.

- **Add value to a sponsorship package.** Add a tagline such as XYZ Bank is a proud sponsor of the ABC Homeless Shelter with a link to the sponsor's website.

- **Save printing and mailing costs.** Trim your mailing list and provide a link to a PDF file of publications on your website.

Change your message frequently to reflect current priorities. Have staff from other departments do the same to communicate multiple messages (e.g.; development department might have a tagline on the annual appeal, while the communications department might have a link to a current news story or new publication).

And keep in mind that, like any good tagline, the message should still be concise. Limit your message to one or two well-worded sentences that include a call to action.

Share Construction Progress With a Webcam

If your organization is undergoing a major construction project, share the progress with a webcam that allows supporters far and wide to follow the project.

Susquehanna University (Selinsgrove, PA) began using a webcam in August 2008 to share progress of a $33-million science building construction project. Paul Novack, director of Web communications, says communications, development and information technology staff began planning for the project six months before construction began.

Novack explains the major goals of the webcam project:

❑ To provide the extended university family the opportunity to follow construction.

❑ To share the progress on the environmentally friendly, state-of-the-art building — the leading priority of the university's Changing Lives, Building Futures capital campaign — with potential donors and persons already partnering with the university.

❑ To obtain images to use for a time-lapse video showing the project from ground breaking to ribbon cutting when the building is complete.

To accomplish these goals, Novack says the university partnered with OxBlue Corporation (Atlanta, GA), a company that provides digital webcam systems specifically for construction projects. He says they chose OxBlue after the chief information officer researched various options. Cost of the project includes a monthly service charge of roughly $500 and an initial hardware investment of more than $3,700.

The image, which refreshes five times each hour, comes from a camera mounted on a building adjacent to the construction project. Novack says elevation and orientation relative to the sun were two considerations in determining where to place the camera. When the project ends, the camera will be added to the campus network of security cameras.

The camera sends images via wireless cellular transmission to OxBlue's Web interface, with an interactive calendar and image zoom features that make the webcam experience more dynamic for website visitors, Novack says.

The university's webcam can be accessed via a link on its news page or directly at this Web address (www.susqu.edu/news/construction/Science_Webcam.htm).

Source: Paul Novack, Director of Web Communications, Susquehanna University, Selinsgrove, PA. Phone (570) 372-4119.

Supporters and potential supporters of a $33 million construction project at Susquehanna University (Selinsgrove, PA) keep tabs on its progress through an online webcam image.

Content not available in this edition

 ## Seven Ways to Attract Blog Traffic

You posted well-written, engaging articles about your organization and its cause. You promote your upcoming fundraiser. You even build a link from your blog to your organization's main giving page, and vice versa.

Don't let these efforts to promote your Web log, or blog, be in vain. Employ these seven steps to boost traffic to your organization's blog:

1. Add your blog to a blog directory such as Nonprofit Blog Exchange, Blogged.com, Blog Catalog or Super Blog Directory.

2. Join Technorati, a blog search engine.

3. Learn how search engines work, and prime your blog for search engine success by using key words and phrases.

4. Make sure your blog is interactive. Offer a RSS feed and allow comments.

5. Be a guest blogger on an established blog. This is a great way to introduce yourself as a blogger and encourage people to visit your blog.

6. Spice up your blog by adding videos and photos.

7. Promote your blog everywhere you can — e-mail signatures, e-newsletters, social networking profiles, business cards, brochures and always-effective word-of-mouth.

Invite Bounce Backs on Your Website

Why ask website visitors for input? To engage them in the work of your organization, obtain their e-mail addresses and gather ideas and opinions, to name a few reasons.

Here are examples of questions/feedback motivators that you may want to include or tailor to fit your organization:

- "The first 50 people to send in correct answers to the following questions will receive a complimentary gift."

- "Do you know the answers to these trivia questions about [name of organization]?"

- "We're looking for examples of... If you can help, please reply."

- "We're taking a vote on this important issue. Please share your response."

- "Do you have news to share for the next issue of our newsletter? Click here to share it with us."

 Market Through Social Media

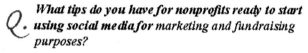

Q. ***What tips do you have for nonprofits ready to start using social media for marketing and fundraising purposes?***

"Keep your expectations low. Twitter won't solve your organization's needs overnight. Assign someone in your organization to be the point for online contact and let employees know about your social media plans, as they may offer ideas and insight. Make sure you have a plan to engage your audience. Use volunteers to further impact your online presence by engaging in social media on behalf of your organization. Don't be afraid to make mistakes. Just start somewhere to begin building your network. It makes much more sense once you start learning about social media."

— Mark Armstrong, Senior Manager,
Internet and New Media,
North Texas Food Bank (Dallas, TX)

"Remember that social media success is all about content. If you have a compelling message, helpful tips and an engaging mission, you'll find a whole lot of people who want to connect with your organization.... Start slowly, setting up a personal Facebook (www.facebook.com) or Twitter (www.twitter.com) account. Get to know how they work, learn how to connect with others and see how other people and organizations are using these tools. Then think about how your content can support your communication strategies, identify your most appropriate spokespeople and establish your organization's online presence. Plan time to keep your accounts up to date, without overdoing it. People like regular updates, but they'll give up on you if your updates are irrelevant, uninteresting or too frequent."

Mark Miller, Director of Philanthropic Marketing &
Communication, Children's National Medical Center (Washington,
DC)

 What's Your Website's Most Important Feature?

Exactly what do you want your website to accomplish?

Whatever the driving force behind your website, visitors to it should be called to action of some sort. Examples of calls to action might include:

- ✓ Requesting additional information.
- ✓ Completing a survey.
- ✓ Signing up for an e-newsletter.
- ✓ Making a contribution.
- ✓ Taking a virtual tour.
- ✓ Becoming a member.
- ✓ Purchasing a product.
- ✓ Submitting opinions/information.

How many times, and in what ways, does your website make calls to action?

 Think Through Anticipated E-mail Campaigns

E-mail campaigns can be highly effective, but they can also be a disaster. Before launching an e-mail campaign answer the following questions:

1. What's the primary purpose of this communication? What do I want it to accomplish?

2. Who am I trying to reach?

3. Why is e-mail the best way to reach this group?

4. What action is the recipient of this e-mail expected to take?

5. How will I handle questions or negative responses?

6. What follow-up should occur when recipients respond?

E-blast Your Chapter Officers

To save time and money, send an e-blast to your chapter's officers.

Sigma Xi: The Scientific Research Society (Research Triangle Park, NC) worked over a three-year period to determine a format that would best fit its target audience. Before 2000, the organization mailed newsletters to chapter officers. As a cost-savings measure, they developed an electronic version of the newsletter, says Katie Lord, director of marketing and communication.

Sigma Xi wanted the e-newsletter to include images in a well-laid out format, but they found those design elements didn't make it to most of the chapter officers, who work in universities and government labs — the attachments and various formats didn't go through spam filters.

After much trial and error, a monthly e-blast is now sent that has a link to a page on the organization's website. There the newsletter is laid out in the format the organization wants.

"They're able to easily access the information with one click," Lord says. "They can cut and paste what they want into an e-mail to their chapter members."

Source: Katie Lord, Director of Marketing and Communication, Sigma Xi, Research Triangle Park, NC. Phone (919) 549-0097. E-mail: klord@sigmaxi.org

 ## E-cards Create Awareness, Engage Online Community

Offering e-cards on your website will engage current users and attract online visitors.

Staff at College of the Holy Cross (Worcester, MA) began offering e-cards on their website in 2000, in part to increase interaction on the site.

"E-cards also help increase awareness of the college," says Christian R. Santillo, interim editor, college Web communications. "Oftentimes people who receive an e-card end up sending one of their own. In the process they're brought back to our website where they can explore other areas."

The college currently offers some 150 e-card designs in 10 categories. "Our most popular card is the squirrel which is part of the campus - today category," says Santillo. "Many of the holiday and commencement cards are also very popular."

Users can send e-cards without having to log in or sign up, making the service an easy and quick way to stay in touch. Plus, the e-cards are free to send and for the college to host, aside from the usual Web hosting fees.

"The e-cards are a great and fun way to send a quick note to a relative or friend for any occasion with a unique Holy Cross twist," says Santillo. "They're popular with alumni who use them to connect with old classmates, and also with prospective students who send them to friends. On campus, faculty and staff use them as thank-you notes to colleagues. Overall, we've found them to be a great way to build community."

The e-cards were created in-house by the Web editors in the public affairs office in collaboration with the Web developers from information technology services. All updates are managed by public affairs.

"In the spring of 2006, the e-cards were redesigned to coincide with a site-wide redesign. At that time, many of the images were refreshed and access to the application was increased," says Santillo. "For example, we included new links to e-cards from several prominent places on the site, including many subsites that are part of our main navigation. This change has enhanced their visibility greatly."

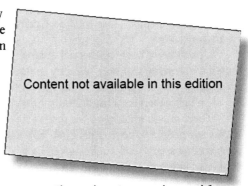

Shown above is a sample e-card from the College of the Holy Cross.

To create personalized e-cards, start with your internal information technology staff. Also, seek input from other like-minded organizations that offer e-cards.

Santillo offers this advice to nonprofits to offer e-cards on their websites:

- You don't need 150 images to get started; 10 to 12 images that showcase your organization is a great place to start.

- Include a logo and create an overall design that coincides with your website and other marketing materials.

- Detailed and clear instructions are a must. Contact information should also be included in case people have problems.

- A great way to increase the use of the application is to debut a new card around a holiday or event.

- When you add a new category, make sure to let people at your organization know.

Source: Christian R. Santillo, Interim Editor, College Web Communications, Office of Public Affairs, College of the Holy Cross, Worcester, MA. Phone (508) 793-2419. Website: http://webapps2.holycross.edu/webapps/ecards/

31   ## Give Colleagues, Staff a Platform to Share Unique Stories

Powerful, memorable stories about your organization often start with the persons who live and breathe your cause.

To encourage colleagues to share story ideas, the communications team at Salve Regina University (Newport, RI) created an Alert the Media website link on its website.

The link encourages students, faculty and staff "to let our office know about some of the off-beat and fun things" they are doing, says Matt Boxler, public information officer, university relations and advancement. "Most often, our university relations office works to publicize lectures, performances, events, etc. Realizing that reporters enjoy writing about interesting people doing interesting things, this was our effort to reach out to our diverse university community to learn about what they were up to."

Boxler came up with the idea after working with a faculty member whose unique hobby drew international media attention. "As a hobby, Dr. Michael DiMaio, professor of philosophy and Latin, runs a website De Imperatoribus Romanis: An Online Encyclopedia of Roman Emperors. Launched in June 1996, his site has surpassed the Oxford Classics Dictionary as the most frequently used reference on all things related to Roman emperors.

"Upon seeing how widespread interest in Dr. DiMaio's unique hobby was, it made sense that we should try to find others in the university community who might have similar stories to tell."

The link generates a handful of submissions each month, he says.

"There are no criteria, as our goal is to encourage people to contact us. That said, many submissions aren't likely to be picked up by media, so rather than turn them down, we make every effort to place them appropriately," Boxler says. "We would try to use these items in the magazine's appropriate sections like Campus News & Notes or Alumni News & Notes, wherever it would fit. Sometimes a submission might only be of interest to the person's hometown newspaper. Other times we might just send a photo opportunity pitch to the local newspaper. The bottom line is that we try to work with each submission to get the biggest splash."

The link brings in tips he and his staff might not otherwise hear about. Boxler says.

"Some of the corresponding coverage we've received has been fantastic, but even if we don't get the big headlines, we consider it a success because we're finding more people to communicate their accomplishments with us."

Source: Matt Boxler, Public Information Officer, University Relations and Advancement, Salve Regina University, Newport, RI. Phone (401) 341-2156.

Website Link Leads To Great Stories

The news article below illustrates the effectiveness of Salve Regina University's Alert the Media website link (detailed at left). Matt Boxler, public information officer, university relations and advancement, explains.

"A faculty member used our Alert the Media to tell us about a student, Leila de Bruyne, who has worked tirelessly to help the children at an HIV/AIDS orphanage just outside Nairobe, Kenya. The By Grace Orphanage is also a school by day to some 120 children. Salve Regina students Justine Axelsson and Leila de Bruyne spent a month volunteering there. Prior to this — de Bruyne's second trip to the orphanage — she raised $15,000 with the help of classmate Bridget Sheerin to benefit the orphanage. They spent the $15,000 on repairs, medical bills, uniforms, books and food. "I splurged on rice, beans and water filters," says de Bruyne. "We took kids to the dentist who never went to the dentist before. When scabies broke out, we bought antibiotics. It was amazing just in a year the changes we made."

Stories about Leila and her classmates were published in their hometown papers, plus the *Providence Journal* and *Newport Daily News*.

Content not available in this edition

Power Your Online Profile for Maximum Success

Online networking can be a cost-effective way to publicize your organization, but only if used wisely. Crafting the right profile can help by doing some of the work for you.

Mandy Wittschen, feature article writer, Haley Marketing Group (Avon, OH), says developing a strong and complete profile allows the site to create the most comprehensive list of contacts for you.

Wittschen recommends including the following items:

✓ Accomplishments and professional background.

✓ Professional and social affiliations.

✓ Current employer (job title, responsibilities, company's line of business).

✓ Work history and education.

When discussing your current employer, include what the business does, who its clients are, its current needs, upcoming events and links to learn more.

Source: Mandy Wittschen, Feature Article Writer, Haley Marketing Group, Avon, OH. Phone (888) 696-2900. E-mail: mwittschen000@centurytel.net

 ## Cut the E-mail Glut

While e-mail can be an efficient tool for distributing messages, its overuse and misuse can lead to apathy and even distrust and low staff morale. Keep these tips in mind to appropriately use e-mail:

- Keep e-mail messages brief. Get to the point. If you need the recipient to respond to three specific questions, indicate so, then number the questions, making it simple to reply to all your issues.

- For persons you contact frequently, ask if they pay more attention to e-mail or voice mail. Note and respect their preferences whenever possible.

- Do not use e-mail to generate ideas, brainstorm or toss up trial balloons when face-to-face or phone conference methods are more effective.

- Use e-mail less and the phone more for one-to-one communication. Where a curt, quickly typed e-mail may unintentionally anger the recipient, a warm voice can quickly soften possible misunderstandings.

- Read incoming e-mails carefully and answer questions so the sender does not have to e-mail again or call to clarify a confusing response. Consider returning an e-mail with a phone call rather than a lengthy written reply.

- End subscriptions to e-mail newsletters that you don't read or use.

- Set and stand by policies restricting company-wide broadcast messages.

 ## Spice Up Your Website With Unexpected Content

Communicating important facts and news updates to your community is always important. And while it's important to provide the public with relevant information, so is offering fresh and interesting facts. You can do this by creating a section on your website that focuses on providing something engaging and unanticipated.

Jon Kavanaugh, director of online content, The Illinois Institute of Technology (Chicago, IL), decided to create a This Month in Tech History section. "In reviewing ways to bring more value to internal and external audiences via the home page, I thought it would be interesting — particularly for students — to see the impact of technological innovation over the years ... kind of the hi-tech equivalent of a word of the day feature."

Whether you decide to create a section that can be updated monthly, weekly or daily, users will appreciate your efforts to provide them with something unexpected. Begin by thinking of innovative ideas and see what might work best for

your website and community. Kavanaugh finds his facts on the Internet as well as from the institute's alumni who have invented products or made major technological innovations.

A major benefit of creating a special fact section on your site is that it will compel users to continue visiting to see what's new. "Having this feature helps frame the institution in the context of innovation and technology development beyond the classroom, something which is part of our primary mission," says Kavanaugh. "These kinds of features are good traffic drivers, improve search engine results and, if done well, give visitors additional reasons to return to the site. I believe nonprofit sites have a built-in opportunity to engage current and prospective audiences with interest-specific features because of their mission-oriented content and services."

Source: Jon Kavanaugh, Director, Online Content, Illinois Institute of Technology, Chicago, IL. E-mail: kavanaugh@iit.edu

35 Document Your Programs With Wide-reaching Videos

Capture the essence of your work by documenting your programs in action.

At Family Health International (FHI), Arlington, VA, "We hire filmmakers to document our activities and produce short video vignettes from that footage," says Steve Taravella, director of communication. "Documentaries are shared with donors, screened in various conference settings and posted online."

The film planning process can take several months. Primary steps include:

- Outlining story — Message, how to deliver it, what images to use, etc.

- Preparing dissemination plan — Who is key audience? What do they need to know? How will they use the film?

- Arranging local site visits and interviews without disrupting program activities.

- Traveling abroad; time spent on the ground and time spent in editing back in the United States.

- Preparing specific script based on images and stories captured.

- Identifying appropriate narration voices once the script is finalized.

- Preparing film draft to screen for relevant staff.

- Making subsequent revisions.

- Dissemination.

FHI films have been shown in global settings such as the 2004 International AIDS Conference, at international meetings and by the U.S. Office of the Global AIDS coordinator at a global conference in 2005. FHI has produced six documentaries since 2001, ranging from eight to 32 minutes, plus shorter vignettes posted on its website.

If considering such a project, Taravella says, realize that documentaries are most effective when they tell a story about a person whose life has been changed. "Don't hit the viewer over the head with the name of the organizations that made it happen. Public relations should be subtle, and shorter is better. Introduce the characters or situation, tell the story and then close."

Source: Steve Taravella, Director of Communication, Family Health International, Arlington, VA.
E-mail: staravella@fhi.org

 ## 36 Don't Forget Your Area Code

In this increasingly global society, assume that more than just local stakeholders are seeing your messages, so don't forget to include your phone number's area code on your website.

 ## 37 Online Pressroom Dos and Don'ts

Creating an online pressroom can be a great asset to your organization, if it's done correctly. Providing the right kind of information and making it user friendly for media contacts researching your organization is essential.

Ellen Davis, senior director of strategic communications, National Retail Federation (Washington, DC), shares her thoughts on the do's and don'ts for online pressrooms:

DO —

1. Make as much information available as possible. Reporters love raw research data and trend information. If you give them information up front, your phone will ring less with information requests.

2. Ensure contact information is very easy to find. Include cell phone information if applicable. Try not to send reporters to a general phone number or e-mail address because those are not always monitored frequently.

3. Keep your website up to date. There is nothing worse than a press release from 2003 hanging around on your site.

4. Include information about spokespeople — their bio and a link to download a high-resolution image.

DON'T —

1. List the contact information for your CEO or other executives unless you're okay with reporters going straight to them.

2. Get too crazy with graphics and design. Links should be clear and easy to find.

3. Forget to spellcheck! There is nothing worse than a press website with misspelled words.

4. Require reporters to register before getting information. They will most likely be turned off and not use you as a resource.

Source: Ellen Davis, Senior Director, Strategic Communications, National Retail Federation, Washington, DC. Phone (202) 783-7971. E-mail: davise@nrf.com

Google Offers In-kind Advertising

Could your organization benefit from free advertising? Check out Google Grants (www.google.com/grants/), an in-kind donation program awarding free AdWords™ advertising to select charitable organizations.

Grant recipients are awarded an in-kind advertising account they may use in a variety of ways: general outreach, fundraising activities and volunteer recruitment. Past recipients' success stories include the USF Fund of UNICEF's e-commerce site, shop UNICEF, which experienced a 43 percent increase in sales over the previous year and CoachArt — a nonprofit supporting children with life-threatening illnesses through art and athletics programs — which has seen a 60 to 70 percent increase in volunteers.

Organizations receiving grants create ads and choose words and phrases related to their cause. When people enter a chosen keyword into the online search engine, Google, the organization's ad appears next to search results and links people to the nonprofit's website.

To learn more, visit Google (www.google.com/grants/details.html).

 ## YouTube Channel Puts University Research Front and Center

How would you like to share your work and get your message out to 500 people a day? That's what a branded YouTube channel (www.youtube.com) is accomplishing for Purdue University (Lafayette, IN), according to Mike Willis, staff member with Purdue's online experience and emerging technologies group, Office of Marketing and Media.

Purdue's public information and media relations staff started using the channel after noticing other research universities — including the University of California, Berkeley — were doing so successfully.

With the help of the public relations office at Berkeley and YouTube staff, Purdue staff created its own presence on the popular video-sharing site.

In most cases, university officials post videos that are produced in conjunction with news releases put out by the university, Willis says. "Other areas of the university provide some material," he says, "but the basic idea is to not put up video that we would be embarrassed to see on the local TV stations."

They include links to the videos in news releases sent to media and published on Purdue's website. A faculty/staff newsletter also lists links to news releases and videos.

Statistics provided through YouTube analytics (which also tell how viewers locate videos and basic demographic information) show Purdue videos are viewed 500 times per day. YouTube also uses Purdue's channel as a good example

> ### Setting Up a Branded YouTube Channel
>
> Thinking about how your organization can get started with YouTube (www.youtube.com)?
>
> The site has a program for nonprofits to create their own branded channels.
>
> The program, for eligible nonprofits in the United States and United Kingdom, provides premium branding capabilities and uploading capacity. It also gives the option to drive fundraising, place a call-to-action overlay on videos and post on the YouTube Video Volunteers' Platform to locate a skilled YouTube user to create your video.
>
> For more information or to get started, plus how to maximize your YouTube channel to benefit your cause, visit www.youtube.com/nonprofits.

of a university channel.

Willis suggests making sure you have a plan for providing updates and new material for the channel if considering pursuing this form of information sharing.

Source: Mike Willis, Online Experience and Emerging Technologies Group, Office of Marketing and Media, Purdue University, West Lafayette, IN. Phone (765) 494-0371. E-mail: jmwillis@purdue.edu

 ## Keep Donor Appeals Above the Fold on Your Website

We've all heard the term above the fold in relation to direct mail, but how does it apply to your website?

On the Internet, above the fold refers to anything viewable on screen without visitors having to scroll down to see it. This information is most pertinent as it applies to your Donate Now button. This is one item on your home page that should definitely be above the fold, large enough and bold enough to be immediately noticed.

Ask some of your current donors to visit your home page and give you feedback on donor appeal, ease of donation and visibility of donor button and information.

41 Image of the Day Draws in Online Visitors

Featuring a new photo on your website every day or so will create anticipation among your users while allowing you to showcase exciting happenings.

Staff at the Woods Hole Oceanographic Institution (Woods Hole, MA) began an Image of the Day website feature in April 2006.

"As a private, nonprofit institution funded largely through public funds, we have an obligation to inform the public about our activities," says Fritz Heide, director of communications. "We also wanted to make our internal audience — the staff — aware of the activities going on all around them.

"Image of the Day is one of the tools we use. A good image attracts attention and tells a story. The captions and links lead to related information on our website, which might be harder to find through conventional navigation," Heide says.

"The initial idea came from the web group manager, who had been featuring a periodically updated slide show on the institution's internal homepage.

"The feedback on the slide show was positive but created a demand for more information about the images — a caption," he says. "We were also beginning to look at RSS feeds and this seemed like a nice feature to provide.

A section featuring a frequently updated image will prompt users to visit your site more often. "We track unique visits periodically," Heide says. "We have roughly 5,300 external subscribers to the RSS feed who have it sent to them automatically each day, and it is featured on the institution's external and internal homepage."

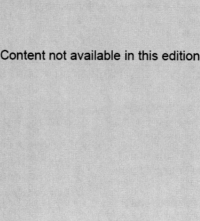

Content not available in this edition

To choose photos for the online feature, they use some archived photos from the institution's extensive image library, plus images taken by staff on research expeditions in the field or at work on shore. "When we launched the Image of the Day project, we promoted the idea to staff," he says, "asking them to submit their favorite images. This turned out to be a good way to collect interesting images."

All the institution's website images are copyrighted by Woods Hole Oceanographic Institution, Heide says, noting that it's important to make sure images you use are not copyrighted by another organization or photographer. "The costs associated with the feature are primarily labor costs," Heide says. "Our media group has a camera loan program to encourage capturing better images. Associated with this program, which predates the Image of the Day, is free training on still cameras and video cameras by our Graphic Services professionals."

Source: Fritz Heide, Director of Communications, Woods Hole Oceanographic Institution, Woods Hole, MA.
E-mail: fheide@whoi.edu

Insight into Creating, Maintaining an Image of the Day Web Feature

Heide offers additional insight into creating and maintaining its daily website photo feature:

Projects Dovetail With Image Feature Launch
As Image of the Day was being created, two converging projects were under way in the communications department that allowed images to be easily extracted from the system and provided a framework to attach captions in advance:

1. **Development of a content management system** to support need to constantly update the institution's web presence and allow updates without having to write code each time.

2. **Creation of an image management system.** With a vendor, they developed a Web-based catalog and download system for the institution's extensive still image library, providing a catalog and archiving system complete with metadata.

Site Maintenance: Two People, 6-10 Hours a Week
Two people are involved in maintaining the institution's Image of the Day website feature. They are:

1. **The image management system manager** (who is also a photographer and graphic services manager) selects, sizes, and puts images into a queue in the content management system as they come in from various sources. A particular image may be sought out to support some event. Average time needed per week: 3-5 hours.

2. **A science writer** who works in public and media relations reviews selected images and metadata and writes captions with links to additional information. He confirms accuracy of information and seeks relevant links. The ability to build up a cache of images with captions in the queue allows this to be done in advance and not interfere with other deadlines.

Think Creatively to Maximize News of Major Achievements

When your nonprofit is recognized for its high level of service or contributions to the community, don't let the publicity end with a news release announcing the honor. Do all you can to spread the news throughout your service region and to your supporters.

While not every award will result in broad media coverage, you can do several things to increase public awareness of your recent achievements. For example:

❑ **Create award icons for Web and e-mail.** Develop a design template for a digital logo like Top 10 Best Hospitals for 2009 or Best Environment for Children with the name of the awarding organization. Use them on your website and in all e-mail communications for a designated period of time, updating as needed.

❑ **Buy advertising or use public service announcements (PSAs).** TV, newspaper or radio advertising is an effective way to thank the organization or people responsible for your success while simultaneously announcing your achievement.

❑ **Target specific reporters.** When a professional group singles out a specific department or service area in your organization for excellence, look to share this good news with the appropriate media outlets. For instance, an Excellence in HR Services honor may make an excellent article for your local business journal or industry trade paper.

❑ **Highlight individuals.** If specific individuals or groups of volunteers were the impetus behind your organization's honor, contact their respective churches, schools or alumni group with the good news. Smaller publications that run once a month or less frequently are often more fully read than daily papers because recipients are targeted.

❑ **Use electronic e-mail services and newsletters.** Services like Constant Contact® (www.constantcontact.com) and Network for Good (www.networkforgood.org) enable you to send attractively presented announcements to large audiences. Include media contacts in your lists, and use attention-getting subject lines like "Selected Among Best Managed Facilities by National Magazine."

❑ **Consider unique advertising methods.** Bus benches, vehicle wraps and billboards can be cost-effective ways to attract positive attention, particularly when your contract permits changing the design or copy as you receive other awards. The brevity of the message Ranked #1 lends itself to a medium people will see while driving or waiting in traffic.

 ## Garner Attention, Online Traffic With Web Spotlight

A web spotlight is an effective way to shine attention on unique departments and units within your organization.

At University of California (Berkeley, CA), Karen Holtermann, executive director, university communications, says: "Our Web Spotlight feature on the UC Berkeley NewsCenter gives us an opportunity to highlight new and content-rich websites within the berkeley.edu domain.

"Berkeley is a huge and decentralized campus, with many units doing interesting work that might not be on the radar of our readers," Holtermann says. "This is one way to introduce those campus units to a broader audience."

Launched in 2003 by the public affairs team, the feature spotlights UC Berkeley entities — departments, units, research centers, etc. — with URLs that end in berkeley.edu.

Choosing what to feature "is purely an editorial decision — what is interesting to us and strategically important to the campus," Holtermann says. "We occasionally receive requests (which are weighed on whether the sites are Berkeley sites, newsworthy, compelling and of general interest), but mostly the ideas come from our own searching or determination to meet a campus need."

Holtermann says they generally change the spotlight once a week, or less frequently to make sure readers have had a chance to see the featured site.

Maintaining the section is done in-house using a template in which they insert a screenshot or other photo, write a blurb describing the site, and add the link.

Check with your IT department for a format that is easy to update and maintain.

Content not available in this edition

Source: Karen Holtermann, Executive Director, University Communications, University of California, Berkeley, CA. Phone (510) 642-0702. E-mail: newscenter@berkeley.edu

44 Offer an Online Diary to Give Members Inside Look

Sharing stories about what's happening at your organization through photos is a great way to keep members connected. Doing so online allows you to bypass any geographic barriers.

One example of this concept in action can be found at www.wlu.edu, the home page of Washington and Lee University (Lexington, VA).

The feature, Scene on Campus, is a slideshow created weekly that contains photos related to the university — sporting events, lectures or just a snapshot that captures the beauty of the campus.

While staff do not currently keep statistics that show how many people visit Scene on Campus online, Jeff Hanna, executive director of communications and public affairs, says the feature does draw attention and generate feedback.

"It's been a very popular feature," Hanna says. "We get feedback all the time from alumni and students that they very much like looking at the photos. It helps bring people back to the time they've spent here."

The slideshows are created with Soundslides (www.soundslides.com), a software program that combines still images and audio, if desired, into a slick slideshow presentation on the Web.

Web editor Jessica Carter, who produces the weekly feature, says most of the effort actually rests on the university's two photographers.

"It only takes me about two hours a week to caption the photos and load them," Carter says. "It takes them about two to five hours each week to choose which photos they want to share and color correct them."

Some past slideshows have even been dedicated to a single subject, such as the renovation of a historic building on campus, complete with blueprints. The slideshows will also feature photos submitted by students, alumni and others.

"It all keeps people engaged with the university," Carter says.

Source: Jeff Hanna, Executive Director of Communications and Public Affairs; Jessica Carter, Web Editor; Washington and Lee University, Lexington, VA. Phone (540) 458-8459. E-mail: jhanna@wlu.edu

 45 Online Auction Benefits School in Several Ways

Many organizations host an annual auction to raise funds for their cause. Take your auction online and raise funds all year long from the global community.

Nicholas Greif, president and CEO, HWXchange online auction (Harvard-Westlake School) of Los Angeles, CA, explains. "Parents are increasingly connected to the Internet through their work and through their children. Thus, moving to an online auction platform is a logical step for nonprofits. People enjoy the added convenience of browsing an auction from home. A nonprofit online auction can also reach a much wider audience. We attracted millions of buyers through the eBay interface."

An online auction is a highly effective fundraising tool and an excellent vehicle for involving students in a business venture. The Xchange has raised roughly $200,000 in two years. "We launched the student-run venture at the start of the 2005-2006 school year and had 15 volunteers by the end of the year. We doubled our staff to 30 student volunteers the following year and added a parent association auction as well," says Greif. "We established a 30-person online auction business in two years, while introducing students to the entrepreneurial process."

As with any fundraising effort, publicity is the key to generating interest.

"We publicized the HWXchange in every possible venue, placing ads in the school newspaper, handing out magnets and flyers at events, adding a link on the school website, and placing bulletins in the parent newsletter," Grief says.

The response has been wonderful. "We have 100 percent positive feedback rating on eBay. The HWXchange is also viewed as a creative and educational venture by the community. Parents donate items to a cause that directly benefits their children and also offers hands-on business experience before they graduate high school."

Source: Nicholas Greif, President and CEO, HWXchange, Los Angeles, CA. Phone (818) 980-6692. E-mail: ngreif@wharton.upenn.edu

---

Coordinating an Online Auction

Greif details the cost involved in creating and maintaining the online auction, saying "Overall, running an online auction is relatively inexpensive. Using eBay is free for nonprofits that register through www.missionfish.org. Additional costs are minimal. We pay for two software programs: one that organizes our listings and coordinates our finances and another that prints USPS postage from our office. Our start-up costs included a camera, lighting and shipping supplies. We pay for advertising (most is free or discounted) and for supplies. We spend $1,000 to $2,000 a year, but easily make back the money we spend."

Webcams Offer Often-visited Window Into Nonprofit's World

Imagine an alumnus in South America logging on to a college's website every morning to watch the sun come up over the campus of his alma mater, or a current student checking from her dorm room to see how long the breakfast line at the dining hall is.

Making both scenarios — and much more — a reality are webcams at Boston College (Chestnut Hill, MA), says Hallie Sammartino, managing director, office of marketing and communications.

Boston College currently has five webcams with real-time video streams throughout campus. The first webcam, launched in 2003, garnered 4,350 hits in four days. The college has since added four more permanent cameras and has even used temporary cameras at their construction sites.

The webcams have generated some 320,000 visits

on bc.edu, and are always in the top 20 for Web traffic, Sammartino says.

Each webcam costs between $1,000 and $2,000, with minimal additional costs for installing and linking them into the college networks, she says, noting benefits far outweigh the costs: "The stories about students calling their parents and jumping up and down in front of the cameras are totally true," she says. "They may be a novelty, but they are one that people enjoy visiting. They offer a real-time perspective for people interested in BC. If we had the resources, we'd definitely get more."

Source: Hallie Sammartino, Managing Director, Office of Marketing and Communications, Boston College, Chestnut Hill, MA. Phone (617) 552-4821. E-mail: sammarha@bc.edu

---

 Hosted Surveys Serve as Communications Tool

Finding ways to get valuable feedback from your community should always be part of your organization's communications strategy. Community surveys are a time-tested way to obtain this feedback.

Surveys can target volunteers, donors and other community members in a way that fits their community involvement. But how do you distribute surveys carefully and efficiently?

Hosted surveys are a great way to develop, gather and review feedback data and won't cost you a lot of manpower. Consider services such as www.surveymonkey.com which allow registered members to create custom surveys that can be easily accessed using a URL you provide to survey participants. The service collects data and provides results in easy-to-read reports. Using this service will save you time and provide your organization with useful information you can use to better your services and programs.

Offer an RSVP by E-mail Option

An RSVP e-mail is a free, easy and efficient way to encourage invitees to respond to event invitations in a timely manner. It allows you to track and save RSVPs and can help decrease follow-up calls.

Gail Bransteitter, communications coordinator, Mercy Housing (Denver, CO) explains. "We give people at least two RSVP options, including phone and e-mail. We created a specific e-mail account that is easy to remember — rsvp@mercyhousing.org. It's highly useful for organizing and tracking our RSVPs. RSVPs received for our events have increased by 15 percent. Using a designated e-mail address saves staff time and make it easier for invitees to respond quickly."

More than 50 percent of Mercy Housing invitees use this option, which is listed on all invitations. "We can organize and track all RSVP e-mails in one place," says Bransteitter.

Source: Gail Bransteitter, Communications Coordinator, Mercy Housing, Denver, CO.

 Simple Show-and-tell Can Add to Your Web Traffic

Everyone knows what donors want, especially in today's economy — results.

Spotlight those results by adding one simple line to thank-you letters, pledge forms, pre-printed receipts and other donor correspondence. For example, staff with the United Way of Snohomish County (Everett, WA) includes

this line on pledge forms and other publications, See how your donation is making an impact at www.uwsc.org.

Regardless of the wording you use, this simple way of connecting your donors to your cause can boost website traffic while feeding your donors what they crave, results.

Learn New Media Tools Before Offering Them to Others

When creating a news-related Web page or revamping your old news page, familiarize yourself with new technologies to ensure you are incorporating the right features.

Recent updates to the website for Swarthmore College (Swarthmore, PA) incorporate the latest technology, says Alisa Giardinelli, associate director of news and information, communications office.

"There was an old news site that served us well, but we wanted to do more. We share the desire to showcase, in a more interactive and dynamic way, the energy and variety of life on campus. Whether it is a Taiko drumming lesson or a lecture on planet formation, in a classroom or on a stage, we want to show in as many ways as possible how life at Swarthmore supports and enriches the life of the mind."

Time spent educating yourself on new media technologies, as well as what other like-minded organizations are incorporating into their news sites, will assist you in the design process and provide you with an arsenal of information.

In the case of Swarthmore's update, "We did some benchmarking of comparable sites and educated ourselves about new media in various ways just to make sure we were on the right track," says Giardinelli.

Benchmarking efforts included participating in a new media workshop organized by the Public Relations Society of America (PRSA); a Bacon's/PRSA webinar; a PRSA teleseminar for counselors to higher education on the topic, The Latest Web Trends for Colleges and Universities, and a CASE-sponsored teleseminar, How New Media Is Changing the Face of University Relations.

The efforts proved beneficial in helping Swarthmore staff create the new site, she says. "They were very useful in orienting us to the landscape and vocabulary of new media."

In additions, a student employed by the news office researched a dozen college news websites, she says. "The student worker surveyed and reported on how new media is used on a number of selective college and university sites around the country. She identified the features she liked and offered her candid opinions about them."

> "Become a user of the kinds of media you want to employ."

Swarthmore staff launched the updated news site in early spring 2008, creating it in-house through a collaborative effort between the news and information office, media services, alumni relations and the information technology department. The new site (www.swarthmore.edu/news) contains videos, podcasts, RSS feeds and blogs.

In determining what to change about the online news page, they also considered carefully what they wanted to stay the same, Giardinelli says.

"We also wanted to keep the best parts of the current site and freshen them up a bit — our sources and experts, news headlines and flagship publications," she says.

Exploring new media technologies first hand is the best way to determine which features will be the most beneficial and effective for your website. "The best advice is to become a user of the kinds of media you want to employ," says Giardinelli. "Short of that, talk — and listen — to people who do."

Source: Alisa Giardinelli, Associate Director of News and Information, Communications Office, Swarthmore College, Swarthmore, PA. Phone (610) 690-5717. Website: www.swarthmore.edu/news

---

 Share Event Information With Online Calendars

Through the online calendar system at http://calendar.google.com, your organization can create a public events calendar that is searchable by millions of users.

By setting up a free account, you can create multiple calendars (events, meetings, etc.). Your calendars can be private or accessible to the public. Once your calendar is public, it is searchable — for instance, a user may search for *heart walk* and the results will allow them to subscribe to the public events calendar of an organization participating in such a walk. Special events from the organization will be automatically saved in the users' personal calendar, keeping them up to date and informed.

 Free Online Press Release Services

If your organization is looking for a fast, free way to distribute press materials, consider using an online press release service. Websites such as www.prleap.com are an effective way to spread your agency's word.

After creating an account, you submit your releases one at a time. On the specified release date of a particular item, the news is released to the public and distributed across the Internet by news syndication services. This method of distributing news online is a great way to generate awareness quickly without having to manually issue releases directly to media outlets yourself.

Because the services are free, you can publish numerous releases, increasing the chances of someone locating your organization's services. Upgraded versions are available for a fee.

53 ## Social Media Strategies That Increase Visibility

Far from being a passing fad, social media is rapidly extending its way into the corporate and nonprofit sectors and changing the way stakeholders communicate with each other, and how they expect to communicate with your organization.

What is social media? It is using the Internet to instantly collaborate, share information and have a conversation about ideas, causes and organizations we care about powered by social media tools (e.g., social networking sites, blogs, podcasts, etc.).

Holly Ross, executive director, NTEN: The Nonprofit Technology Network (Portland, OR), says nonprofit communicators must understand how social media's newfound popularity will impact their cause and relay that to their constituency.

"As nonprofits, we're used to being authorities to our communities," Ross says. "Our role has been to decide what's important regarding our issues, to tell our community what matters, and to organize them to create change."

But the development of the Internet has forced nonprofits to change how they relate to their communities, she says. "First, the Internet has made accessing information incredibly easy. If you want to know about logging in your state, Google will tell you what's going on. Second (and this is the newest part), the Internet has made it ridiculously easy for us to share that information with each other, and to organize around that information.

"What that means is that people don't need us to tell them what matters. They don't need us to organize them. So as nonprofits our value proposition has shifted. We need to learn how they are using these tools to organize themselves, and what they are saying about our issues so we can understand what value we can bring to them."

Ross emphasizes that nonprofit communicators should think of social media as a series of steps that must be taken to increase visibility:

1. **Listen and participate in conversations that are already happening.** First, find out and listen to what people are talking about regarding the issues about which you care. How are they talking about the issues? What's motivating them? Next, use that knowledge to share your own insights and resources.

2. **Share your story.** Once you have a feel for the conversation, get your own story out there via blogs, podcasts, videos, etc. and invite the community to participate. Be brave and create content that is appropriate for your audiences and encourages feedback and conversation.

3. **Generate buzz.** Use sites like Facebook, StumbleUpon, Digg and Twitter to tell the world about what you're up to. Build a community of peers on these sites that will help you get the word out about your stories to their networks.

"The key to all these is community," says Ross. "You have to build real relationships with real people to make it work. That means that you'll have to contribute as much as you take, and you'll have to be open to whatever the community wants to tell you."

Source: Holly Ross, Executive Director, NTEN: The Nonprofit Technology Network, Portland, OR. Phone (415) 397-9000. E-mail: holly@nten.org

---

Social Media's Challenges

Like many forms of communication, social media has its pros and cons, says Holly Ross, executive director, NTEN: The Nonprofit Technology Network (Portland, OR).

Ross offers an example of how social media has changed communications for the better in terms of speed and scope: "We always wanted to create that perfect viral e-mail that would get forwarded around the Web. Adding 25 people to an e-mail send list is tedious compared to adding a link to Digg (www.digg.com). Getting your networks to tell a friend is all about capitalizing on their emotions in the moment. The easier that is, the more you'll get out of it. And social media makes it very easy."

While social media has helped in this manner, she notes it isn't a panacea. Its pitfalls include:

✓ **Presenting challenges to an organization's many cultures.** "To successfully implement a social media strategy, your organization must be prepared to behave in new ways. You have to be much more open and transparent than many organizations have been up to this point. The idea of accepting comments on a blog is abhorrent to many organizations, for example. They can't bear the idea of someone saying something negative."

✓ **Lack of control.** "The biggest mistake I see organizations make is the attempt to control their social media strategy too much. That's not how social media works. You can't delete negative comments. You have to respond to them honestly and openly."

✓ **Social media structure versus organizational structure.** "We're used to working in departmental silos; program does program work, fundraising raises money, marketing tells our stories. Social media combine elements of all of those.... The folks implementing social media strategies are crossing departments more frequently, challenging our old ways of getting work done."

Weigh the Benefits of Electronic Business Cards

Sharing your business card is a great way to network and make new contacts. However the cost of constantly having to order new business cards when your contact information changes can outweigh the benefits. Consider using electronic business cards (vCards). These cost-effective e-mail attachments can be updated automatically and can be easily distributed to your contacts.

Many e-mail programs, such as Microsoft Outlook, have the capability of creating and sharing electronic business cards, giving you a multitude of color and design options that can be updated as needed. Outlook users have the option of creating a card template that can be used by an entire organization for a uniform look.

Outlook lets you add electronic business cards to your e-mail signature. The card can be downloaded by your contacts upon receipt. Not only can you share your business card with more contacts, but you can create different versions of your card for different communication purposes.

Other e-mail programs, such as Mozilla Thunderbird and the Mac OS X mail program, also can create and receive electronic business cards. Talk to your IT department to see if your organization can use electronic business cards.

 ### Seek E-mail Addresses From Newsletter Recipients

Are you considering offering an electronic newsletter to donors, constituents or other key audiences soon? Now's the time to start gathering e-mail addresses.

Even if you plan to keep sending traditional paper newsletters through regular mail, gathering e-mail addresses for those on your mailing list is a good idea. You could use e-mails to test online solicitations, newsletters or as a means to invite supporters to special events.

Here are three ways to start gathering e-mail addresses:

1. Include a call to action in your current newsletter to send an e-mail to be entered in a contest, seek important information — or better yet, receive a free gift.

2. When registering people for special events or fundraisers, ask for their e-mail addresses as well.

3. On your website, prominently feature a button that says Yes, I want to get the latest information by e-mail that links to a simple sign-up form.

 ### Share Important News Quickly With RSS Feeds

Hosting RSS feeds on your website will enable you to spread important news updates and other information quickly and efficiently.

"RSS is a form of syndication of Web content that is used to publish frequently updated content such as blog entries, news headlines, event listings, etc.," says Joe Hunter, assistant vice president for external relations, director of communication, Franklin W. Olin College of Engineering (Needham, MA). "RSS makes it possible for people to keep up with their favorite websites by receiving a feed from sites they have subscribed to using software called a feed reader or aggregator."

RSS feeds can be utilized by any organization wishing to spread news and updates quickly to their constituents. "The idea to implement RSS feeds was discussed in a committee we formed last year to discuss improvements to our website. We had been looking for ways to push information out to our various constituencies, and RSS feeds seemed like the perfect solution," says Hunter. "Once we had implemented them, we made people aware of them through our usual vehicles (e.g., the website, communications with alumni and parents, etc.).

Subscribing to an RSS feed is easy and doesn't require any specialized equipment. "Users can subscribe to RSS feeds using a variety of methods. The OlinFeeds website provides directions that allow people to subscribe to feeds using FireFox 2 and Internet Explorer 7 (Web browsers that provide built-in RSS functionality). There are many news aggregators (software used to read RSS feeds) available, but generally, a user needs an aggregator and the URL containing the RSS feed.

"I think it has benefited our organization by keeping our constituencies better informed about the college and closer to developments here. This could eventually have implications for fundraising and corporate outreach, although the service is too new to make that determination now."

Hunter says when the RSS feed was created at Olin, the project was completed in about 80 hours, which included application requirements, coding, testing and debugging. The main cost was incurred by the organization because the application was developed in-house.

Source: Joe Hunter, Assistant VP for External Relations, Director of Communication, Franklin W. Olin College of Engineering, Needham, MA. Phone (781) 292-2255. Website: www.olin.edu

E-mail Your Board and Volunteer Leadership

To better connect your volunteers and board members with your organization, send them e-mail updates when you make the news. They often don't see news accounts you've helped create and it lets them know of your efforts.

Direct them to a news story on a newspaper website or add a link to news video on TV. As part of relationship building with your board members, volunteers and others, it's a win-win situation.

 Recognition Just a Click Away

For an easy, inexpensive way to secure meaningful recognition for staff or volunteers, do as Rady Children's Hospital (San Diego, CA) does, add a Send a Thank-You button to your website's home page.

Clicking on the hospital's online link leads to a simple online form where patients, their families and others can send a personal message or compliment recognizing an employee's good work.

The tool is an added benefit for patients and consumers too, giving them an opportunity to share their feelings about their experiences at the hospital.

 Eight Tips for Writing Engaging Website Copy

Whether launching a new website or redesigning an existing one, keep some key tips in mind when developing the all-important copy that will fill your Web pages.

Joyce Remy, senior editor with the communications firm, IlluminAge (Seattle, WA), offers information that can help nonprofits create website content that both meets the needs of Web users while getting the most value from their website investment:

1. **Consider the other reader — the search engine.** For search engines to find website pages, the pages must include keywords likely to be used by people trying to find your organization. If your organization is a food bank, use terms on your site such as feeding the hungry and food shelf. "As you craft copy, it is important that your keywords sound natural to the readers," says Remy. "If it looks like you've seeded your text with keywords, your site will seem less trustworthy."

2. **Web users are usually seeking a particular piece of information.** Unlike a brochure or ad, websites come with high expectations as an information source, Remy says. "Tailor your language accordingly, offering customers concrete facts, engagingly presented, about all the services your organization offers."

3. **Users navigate your site in a non-linear fashion.** Because Web users can move freely through the site, it is vital that your text doesn't depend on information found on previous pages. Make a good impression on every page, realizing that page users may arrive on a page other than your home page as they navigate the Web.

4. **Persons read Web pages differently than they read other types of copy.** Remy says studies indicate website visitors usually begin with a quick initial once-over when visiting a page. Visual cues such as short paragraphs, bullet points, subheads and white space ensure they can find what they want quickly.

5. **Compared to the printed page, reading on a computer screen is hard work.** As you begin constructing your text, write long and edit to short. Once capturing your basic points, you can usually trim quite a bit and not lose the meaning. The recommended length for most Web pages is 200 to 400 words per page.

6. **The text of your website doesn't stand alone.** Elements such as logo and contact information, images, navigation buttons and consistent footers allow users to quickly figure out what is available on the site and constantly interact with your text. This can help keep copy concise.

7. **Hyperlinks add a new dimension.** This option allows readers to go to a different spot on the page, different page on your site or to another site entirely. "Hyperlinks give your users the choice of learning about something in greater depth, but don't overdo it," Remy says. "Links can be distracting and once readers leave a page, they may not return." Instead, embed links in a natural fashion. Avoid using click here.

8. **Use website content area wisely.** Dedicate time to work on the copy, hire a copywriter or ask colleagues and clients for feedback, suggests Remy. "Viewers may not know about your organization. Be clear, concise and thorough when describing the services, geographic areas served and your organization's history, staff or philosophy."

Source: Joyce Remy, Senior Editor, IlluminAge Communication Partners, Seattle, WA. Phone (800) 448-5213. E-mail: joyce@illuminage.com

Cut Costs by Moving Annual Report Online

As printing costs continue to rise, more nonprofits are seeking alternative ways to reduce marketing expenditures. From newsletters to magazines to save-the-date cards, more and more communication pieces are moving from people's mailboxes to their e-mail inboxes.

Annual reports are no exception.

Mimi Koral, director of alumni communication, University of Pittsburgh (Pittsburgh, PA), says her office decided to abandon printing annual reports in 2004 after determining that the nearly $65,000 being spent on printing and mailing an annual report was not justified.

"We weren't able to get a good gauge on whether we were getting the attention we were paying for," says Koral. "That's when we decided to go online only."

For two years, these online reports, which Koral describes as elaborate, featured messages from the chancellor and executive director; videos of students talking about the impact of scholarships in their lives; illustrated old and new Pitt traditions; and offered information on faculty projects and volunteer efforts.

"Going online with our annual report gave us the chance to shine light on all these aspects at the same time," says Koral.

In 2006, they replaced the online annual report with an online streaming video of the chancellor's talk.

"After producing the first two online annual reports, we learned constructing the annual reports really ate up our webmaster's time," Koral says. "We realized our chancellor was touching on almost all the major points made in the annual report during his videotaped messages to alumni, so we decided to go with his talk only."

Koral's staff tapes the chancellor's five-minute talk in-house at a total production cost of about $7,500.

Koral publishes its Web page address in the university's paper publications and provides a link via the association's website. Alumni e-mail addresses are gathered from an online alumni directory and a company that searches public databases and matches e-mail addresses to alumni for whom the university does not have an e-mail address.

Source: Mimi Koral, Director of Alumni Communication, University of Pittsburgh, Pittsburgh, PA. Phone (412) 383-7078. E-mail: mimi.koral@ia.pitt.edu

 ## 10 Things to Include in an Online Press Room

If you haven't already established an online press room for your organization, or if yours is in need of updating, here's a checklist of must-have elements:

1. **News Releases** — Post headlines as hyperlinks to articles; list chronologically by most recent news first; include archive of past articles.

2. **Media Updates/What's New!** — Articles spotlighting the latest happenings at your organization or in the community that involve your organization.

3. **FAQ for the Media** — A question-and-answer format addressing commonly asked questions and facts about your organization.

4. **Media Alerts/Sign Up Now!** — Media and others opt to receive updates and news releases automatically by e-mail and/or postal service.

5. **Media Contacts** — Full, 24/7 contact information for the organization's media contact(s).

6. **Upcoming Events** — At-a-glance list of your calendar of fundraisers, community meetings, volunteer recognition events and other happenings; hyperlink to details about each event.

7. **Ask Our Experts** — Expertise directory identifying and providing contact information to staff/volunteers who can speak on specific issues (update to reflect current local, regional, national and international news topics).

8. **[Name of Organization] in the News** — Clips of links to regional and national news coverage of your organization.

9. **Graphics You Can Use** — Downloadable photos/logos/illustrations/documents in .jpg, gif, PDF, .doc, PowerPoint, other typically requested formats.

10. **Accessibility** — Assembling the above information is useless if your online press room is difficult to navigate. Journalists have deadlines. They want information now Making your site as simple to navigate and as comprehensive as possible will increase the chances of reporters coming back.

> **Online Pressroom Examples**
>
> Thomas More College of Liberal Arts — www.thomasmorecollege.edu/page_id=259
>
> Valley CAN — www.valley-can.org/news_photos
>
> Foundation Center — http://foundationcenter.org/media
>
> Mississippi Development Authority — http://pressroom.mississippi.org

Four Questions to Ask to Determine Web Content

If you plan to launch a new or redesigned website, an important first step is determining your website's content.

To give Web planners a starting point, Dennis Kenny, president, IlluminAge Communication Partners (Seattle, WA), and staff developed a Web content and functionality checklist (shown below).

While they originally created the checklist to aid health-care and aging services providers and associations, Kenny says the checklist can guide Web planning for any nonprofit agency.

"Our checklist is just a convenient jumping-off point," he says. "It probably won't include every possible form of content or functionality you'd like to consider, but it will name most of them and serve as a starting point."

The list names more than 25 features to consider when designing a website.

To aid in your website design or re-design project, Kenny shares four questions to help determine what to include as content and online functionality:

1. **Who is our audience?** Because every organization is different, the Web planner needs to begin with a clear appreciation of who the website is meant to serve.

2. **How will they use our website?** To help determine what content will be featured on your website, a successful website should be audience-driven. "A successful website is one that responds as directly as possible to what the website's users need, want and value," says Kenny.

3. **Is it in our budget?** While online content and functionality are less expensive than their print and in-person counterparts, they still come with a price. Kenny recommends asking your Web developer for a cost breakdown and the flexibility to include some elements now, and defer others until later. Kenny says it is also important during website design to plan for future growth as the audience's needs and expectations evolve.

4. **Can we keep it current?** Does your organization have the horsepower (e.g., staffing, volunteers, budget) to maintain the content you seek to include? "Better to leave it out," he says, "than to put it in and have it go stale because no one is available to keep it current."

Source: Dennis Kenny, President, IlluminAge Communication Partners, Seattle, WA. Phone (800) 448-5213, ext. 303. E-mail: dennis@illuminAge.com

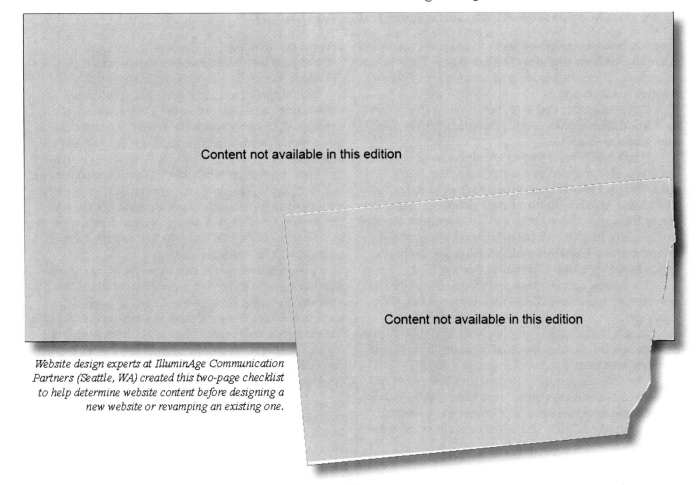

Content not available in this edition

Content not available in this edition

Website design experts at IlluminAge Communication Partners (Seattle, WA) created this two-page checklist to help determine website content before designing a new website or revamping an existing one.

10 Steps to Craft a Sponsor-friendly Website

Your organization's website can be a powerful tool in securing sponsors for your events and campaigns, but only if it's got the right stuff. Consider and craft the following items in order for your website to be sponsor-friendly:

1. Make sponsor information easy to find. Put a sponsor information tab on your home page or a large block asking the question, "Interested in becoming a sponsor?" For an even stronger start, tie the question directly to the people you serve (e.g., Interested in helping to feed children? Interested in sending sick kids to camp?)

2. Make contact information clear and easy to find. Some people interested in becoming sponsors may only glance at the information on the site, preferring to follow up by phone or e-mail. Make doing so a no-brainer.

3. Think of what questions a sponsor might ask, then answer them in a frequently asked question (FAQ) section.

4. Be specific as to why sponsors should care about your organization and how sponsorships benefit them as well.

5. List who else sponsors you. In the business community that can make a difference.

6. Include in your online sponsor list any logos and links to your sponsors' websites.

7. Talk generally about why your organization is relevant to the community at large and the persons you reach through demographics. If your organization appeals to families of children age 6 to 12, that may be important to businesses trying to reach those groups.

8. Include testimonials from other sponsors and the people you serve. Consider using video or audio clips.

9. Issue a specific call to action. What is the next big thing coming up that needs sponsorship? What current services need to be fulfilled to allow you to fulfill your mission? Include a list of annual events in need of sponsors.

10. Include a detailed list of all opportunities you have available for sponsors and how to take the next step.

 Flickr Provides Photo Storage and Sharing Options

Looking to share your photos with a widespread community? Online photo management applications such as Flickr (http://flickr.com) offer both free and paid accounts that allow you to store and share photos.

Communications staff at Medaille College (Buffalo, NY) purchased a Flickr pro account in December 2007 to store and publish their photos.

"I had used (Flickr) for personal photos under a different account and appreciated how easy it was to use. I also admired how Flickr has built in new tools and features," says Kara Kane, assistant director of communications. "After we set up the account, I was shocked to see how high it appeared in Google rankings for Medaille College, it's been as high as number five. That alone made us realize that prospective students and our alums might find us this way."

The college currently has about 500 pictures in the Flickr pro account, which costs $24.95 for one year or $47.99 for two years.

Images in Medaille's Flickr account include photos from commencement. Pictures are added to the Flickr account several times per month.

"We add images and link to them from news posts and in e-mail newsletters to alumni," says Kane. "With Flickr we can create badges based on sets of images that are easy to insert into static HTML pages on our main site or into news items on our news site."

Kane and her staff take several steps to let the Medaille community know about the online photos.

"I've started to add a link to our Flickr account on press releases that I send out," she says. "The link is on our news site and will be on our sports site as well. In addition, I will start to post a message through Facebook as I post new sets of images."

Kane and staff use Flickr mostly for sharing photos and as a secondary storage space for some images. Most photos are backed up on a shared storage drive and CD, she says. "Eventually, I'd like to see us rely on Flickr for more of our photo storage needs, publishing the best content and maintaining it with informational captions.

"For organizations that lack, as we do, a fulltime programmer with the ability to create functional slideshows for mass use, a site like Flickr makes it easy for a non-Web-savvy individual to create professional-looking sets of images that can have a wide reach," Kane says. "By implementing features like the RSS feeds for pictures too, and integrating the pictures into a main website, you can complement your news and events with images for your audience."

Source: Kara Kane, Assistant Director of Communications, Medaille College, Buffalo, NY. Phone (716) 880-2884. Website: www.medaille.edu

65 Display Accomplishments Prominently Online

Highlighting accomplishments on your website is a notable way to share these facts with internal and external audiences.

Staff at Mississippi State University (Starkville, MS) created the online feature, Points of Pride, to showcase brief, newsy bragging points about the university, says Maridith Geuder, director, university relations. For instance, a recent point of pride spotlighted the fact that Kiplinger's Personal Finance magazine named Mississippi State among its 100 Best Values in Public Colleges.

"Points of Pride originated as a (Microsoft) Word-based document that we shared around campus, and has since migrated to an online version," Geuder says. "Our Web developers created a database that is updated by one of our university relations editors to highlight information related to student, faculty, athletic and alumni accomplishments."

Created more than a decade ago, the feature is updated by Kay Jones, publications editor, university relations.

"I get material from our news releases, although sometimes I take items from publications we produce," Jones says. "Obviously, you pick topics that you are proud of and want to share with the public. It's not really very hard to select once you keep that in mind."

Individual items in the Points of Pride database rotate randomly on the Alumni and Friends Web page and are linked on the president's Web page, says Geuder. "Because of the multiple uses, we feel we've increased opportunities to highlight Mississippi State's accomplishments through this single project."

When compiling information for an online spotlight, consider borrowing from other departments or sharing your database with colleagues who develop speeches or promotional materials.

Information used in the university's online feature, Geuder says, is often the basis for public presentations, such as alumni meetings and talks to civic groups about Mississippi State, and provides information for talking points.

Sources: Maridith Geuder, Director; Kay Fike Jones, Publications Editor; University Relations, Mississippi State University, Starkville, MS. Phone (662) 325-3442. E-mail: geuderm@ur.msstate.edu or jonesk@ur.msstate.edu

66 Offer Online Registrations

Providing online event or open house registrations streamlines the process for staff and provides an easy option for persons interested in attending the event.

Offering online registrations for open houses at Frostburg State University (Frostburg, MD) simplifies the process for everyone involved, says Wray Blair, associate vice president for enrollment management.

"It is much easier than placing a form in the mail or making a phone call," and available 24 hours a day, Blair says. "We've been offering online registration since 2004 and have found that it is the preferred method of registration for our families."

Online Form Triggers Confirmation

The registration form asks for student name, birth date, phone, e-mail and mailing addresses, high school or college, intended major, intended enrollment term and total number of people attending the open house.

Once submitted, the form is automatically e-mailed to the campus visit coordinator, who officially registers the student for the program. The student receives immediate e-mail confirmation. The visit coordinator enters the online registration into a database, which automatically generates a label to mail confirmation and itinerary to the student.

Eliminating Paper Form Headaches

The online method also eliminates having to struggle with multiple paper forms or try to decipher handwriting.

"Our staff is really pleased with the ease of the online registration process," says Blair. "It works well for our prospective students and it works well for our office."

The process also provides a more convenient way to communicate with prospective students and families, Blair notes. "In the very competitive world of college admissions, it is vital to always provide the highest level of customer care. We have found that approximately 80 percent of our open house visitors utilized the online registration option."

Source: Wray Blair, Associate Vice President for Enrollment Management, Frostburg State University, Frostburg, MD. Phone (301) 687-4401. E-mail: wnblair@frostburg.edu

67 **Twitter Generates a Buzz Over Event**

Toronto's techie community banded together to organize Ho-HoTO (Toronto, Canada) using Twitter (www.twitter.com) as the driving force to generate buzz about the December 2008 event, which drew the attention of the technology, marketing and public relations professional communities and raised $25,000 for the local food bank.

Michael O'Connor Clarke, vice president of Thornley Fallis Communications (Toronto, Ontario, Canada), talks about HoHoTO and how it became a success with less than two weeks of planning:

How many people attended the event?
"There have actually been two HoHoTO events. The first in December 2008, and a recent summer party we threw together on a whim in August. Pronounced 'hoe hoe TEE oh' — the T.O. stands for the affectionate local nickname for Toronto, 'the big T.O.' — the first event drew close to 650 people raising $25,000 in just a little more than 15 days of planning. The August event drew 500 and raised $13,000."

To whom and how many was information transmitted via Twitter?

"It's really hard to say how many people we reached through Twitter. We sent out simple messages to let friends and followers know we were working on this insane plan to host a huge charity party, with about 15 days of prep time. Our friends helped spread the word. Friends of friends spread it further.

"This is the network effect of Twitter at its best. From initial messages posted to Twitter by a handful of us, it went viral. At a couple of points in the run-up to the first event, and on the night of the event itself, the name of the event was the top trending topic on Twitter. Trending topics are Twitter's way of tracking big news items and other daily themes that emerge when a large group of people online are all talking about the same thing. People logging into the main Twitter home page or using one of a number of the popular third-party Twitter tools would have seen the HoHoTO topic rising to the top. Many Twitter users then asked on Twitter what HoHoTO was, further spreading the word."

Why was the Twitter marketing campaign so successful?
"First, the group of people behind HoHoTO are well-connected people in the Toronto (and broader) online community, yet each of us also has a particular area of influence. One of the key HoHoTO team members and our de facto leader, for example, is Rob Hyndman, a technology lawyer. I've been in the tech business my entire life, and know many of the people Rob knows in Toronto and elsewhere, but we also have big networks that don't overlap.

"Our organizing team included a diverse group of people — including the nonprofit sector, professional photography community, music business professionals and many more — with big personal networks and local influence among certain related but very different communities. The only thing we had in common is that we are all enthusiastic social media users, big Twitter fans and self-confessed geeks. This set of connections helped us spread the word far and fast.

"Secondly, the idea. I think we just struck a chord. Toronto was in the thick of the downturn and in that grey, miserable, not-quite-winter time of the year. People wanted an excuse to party and celebrate the vibrant geek community in Toronto.

"Third, the cause. There had been quite a bit of news about the plight of the local food banks in the run-up to the holidays. This galvanized us and made it easy to get powerful messages of need across to the community."

How much potentially was saved by marketing via Twitter versus standard marketing methods?
"Thousands. We did no real marketing at all. We used e-mail among team members, a Google Groups setup (like an instant Intranet) and Twitter as our communications tools, marketing channels and project management essentials. There were some costs involved in staging the event, but we managed to convince almost everyone to give us their services or products for free as in-kind donations."

Source: Michael O'Connor Clarke, Vice President, Thornley Fallis Communications, HoHoTO, Toronto, Ontario, Canada. Phone (416) 471-8664. E-mail: mocc@thornleyfallis.com

68 **Six Ways to Help Users More Easily Navigate Your Website**

No matter how good your website content may be, if visitors to your site can't find it, it's of no use to them and of no benefit to you. Here are six ways to help users more easily navigate your website:

1. Keep navigation link titles short but descriptive.

2. Don't include too many links from your main page. If your website contains more than six to seven pages, include the remaining links on secondary pages.

3. Offer a text alternative to pages with lots of graphics.

4. Make sure users can tell whether the link has already been clicked.

5. Create a site map or contents page so users can easily find sought-after information.

6. Keep the main menu visible and accessible on each page so that users can navigate throughout the main pages of the site from any page they may be reading.

69 Pique Interest in What Others Are Saying

When your organization gets a positive plug in the media, tell others about it.

Dickinson College (Carlisle, PA) has a "What They're Saying" heading on the home page followed by a teaser that reads: "A national magazine cited Dickinson as a college that compares favorably with the 'gotta-get-in' schools. Who said this about us?" Persons who click the link are directed to the college's media page, complete with information about recent mentions of Dickinson in Time, Men's Fitness, The Atlantic Monthly and The Wall Street Journal.

Don't think that you have clips worth mentioning? What is considered prominent is relative to the size of your media market and scope of your organization. Any favorable mention in the press will help bolster your legitimacy with prospective donors.

Source: Karen Neely Faryniak, Associate Vice President for College Relations, Dickinson College, Carlisle, PA. Phone (717) 245-1578. E-mail: faryniak@dickinson.edu

70 iTunes Service Provides More Than Just Music

Harness the popularity and availability of the well-known iTunes music service for massive multimedia distribution. For example, using the iTunes U and mobile learning service, educators can publish multimedia such as audio and video recordings that students and other users can download through iTunes software.

At Seattle Pacific University (Seattle, WA), "We primarily use iTunes U as a way to repurpose audio and video content from an on-campus event to an audience that wasn't able to attend and/or those who were able to participate live and want to hear or watch it again or recommend it to others," says David Wicks, director, instructional tech. "We also have faculty and staff who record original content and distribute it to students through iTunes U" and record podcasts for incoming students and their parents.

University officials began using iTunes U in 2005 after Apple Inc.'s then-new iTunes U project involving five institutions. "We kept our eyes on that project and sent our application in right away when Apple opened it to other institutions in 2006," Wicks says. "We needed a system that was easy to use, inexpensive and didn't require a lot of interaction with our IT people. Apple's iTunes U met all of our requirements."

Currently, the university has 3,000 audio and video files available, the largest being their chapel speakers section. "We have chapels dating back to 1970," says Wicks. "We frequently hear from alumni who are able to relive a bit of their past by listening to a lecture they heard while in school."

Instructional tech staff and students maintain the iTunes feature.

"The content providers (lecturers) provide the original metadata that is associated with each file," says Wicks. "Staff and students in our office verify this information, and update the iTunes U Store page

on a regular basis."

The iTunes U feature has proven to be tremendously popular with the university community. "We are currently averaging about 40,000 downloads a month," says Wicks. "In April 2007 we were averaging 1,000 downloads a month." The university has a page on its website dedicated to iTunes U (www.spu.edu/itunes).

As for costs associated with the iTunes feature, he says, "Apple does not charge for hosting the content so we don't have server or hosting costs, and most of the content is repurposed so there is minimal cost in production. Now that we have all of our archived materials online, we include iTunes production as part of our regular process when creating content.

"iTunes U has been an effective tool for creating awareness of lectures and other events on our campus," Wicks says. "I don't think it has had a negative impact on attendance; rather, we see those who attended want to listen/ watch again to pick up something missed the first time."

Source: David Wicks, Director, Instructional Tech, Seattle Pacific University, Seattle, WA. Phone (206) 281-2290. Website: www.spu.edu/itunes

Content not available in this edition

Pay-per-click Advertisements Increase Visibility

Pay-per-click advertising allows you to target a specific audience while drawing more users to your website.

One nonprofit organization seeing positive results from this form of online advertising is the University of Colorado Hospital (UCH) in Aurora, CO.

"Our main strategic goal — and the bulk of our resources — of our current campaign are devoted to raising public awareness of our hospital," says Bill Sonn, director, marketing and public relations. "As we proceed, however, we wanted to develop effective direct marketing tools for our best-known services in cancer, transplant, neurosciences and stroke care, and heart. With our advertising agency, we determined that learning more about pay-per-click advertising would be important.

"Our pay-per-click ads appear on search engine results pages. They promoted four specific service lines: cancer, transplant, neurosciences and cardiac," Sonn says. "When people used certain search terms, UCH would show up at or near the top of the paid messages on the right side of the results page.

"We kept track of which search terms worked best, and changed out the ones that didn't work well. We graded how well they worked by how many visits to our site they evoked, and how long people stayed on our site."

A pay-per-click campaign can involve providing a search engine with your text block or image ad. When users search online for related material, the search engine includes your ad in results. If users click on your ad, you pay a predetermined amount.

UCH began using pay-per-click ads in February 2006 and continues to utilize them.

"We've gotten literally tens of thousands of additional click-throughs to our site (see Numbers Show Ads' Effectiveness, at right), most emanating from people with a precise interest in the specific information and care we're attempting to deliver," Sonn says. "Moreover, we can tell how long they spend on our site, where they tend to go on it, etc. At minimum, it's been a terrifically successful experiment."

Prices for this type of advertising can vary greatly.

"In health care it is more expensive, for example, to do pay-per-click for cardiac care than it is for, say, solid organ transplant," he says. "Bariatric surgery and refractive surgery also are relatively pricey. The reason has more to do with competition than it does with acuity or even quality of care. There are many more private businesses competing for patients in those areas, and they drive up the price the rest of us have to pay for each click."

If you do not have access to an advertising agency, online resources are available to set up pay-per-click ads, such as Google AdWords (www.google.com/intl/en/ads/) and AdBrite (www.adbrite.com).

For UCH, Sonn says, they used Denver-based Cactus Communications (www.sharpideas.com). "Cactus Communications was really the knowledge source for all this. It helped identify strategy and media buys, did the production, brought us suggestions for mid-course corrections, etc. We were intimately involved in messaging as well as all the steps along the way."

Pay-per-click ads are an eye-catching way to attract targeted users to your organization's website, he says. "They've helped us shape strategies to get people to our site, and ultimately to navigate through our site to the pages we want them to reach. We were able to distinguish how people get to us through pay-per-click, and how people who do organic searches — e.g., without using pay-per-click — get to us."

Sonn recommends other nonprofits consider pay-per-click advertising. "It's a promising way to reach precise audiences."

Source: Bill Sonn, Director, Marketing & Public Relations, University of Colorado Hospital, Aurora, CO. Phone (720) 848-7810.

Numbers Show Ads' Effectiveness

Bill Sonn, director, marketing and public relations, University of Colorado Hospital (UCH), shares statistics showing the impact of pay-per-click advertising on website traffic:

- 18,520 page views of various cancer pages from 7,993 visitors; 13,744 of those were unique views.

- Viewer average of 1.32 minutes on a page. About 54 percent left the site after viewing one page.

- Most frequently viewed page — Contact us.

- 53 percent of all visitors to the UCH website came to the site directly, not from another site or from a search engine; 11 percent came from referring sites; 35 percent from search engines.

- Top referring site: University of Colorado Health Sciences Center, followed by University of Colorado Hospital.

- Top key words in above-mentioned time period: chest cancer; University of Colorado Hospital; Anschutz cancer center; gu cancer and university hospital.

72 News Blog Invogorates Online Newsroom

Go beyond a typical blog to start a news-specific blog for your online newsroom.

"We created the Babson College news blog in March 2006," says Michael Chmura, director of public relations, Babson College (Babson Park, MA). "Different individuals gather information through different methods — some prefer text, others video and others audio. The blog reaches that audience.

"In addition, we saw the blog as a flexible tool to deliver news that doesn't fit the traditional press release format: interviews, business profiles, conference coverage, etc.," says Chmura.

"The blog allows us to distribute information immediately," he says. "We can attend a presentation and post from the room. We can liven up coverage of events, like our student business fair, with multiple photos of the teams. In many ways it serves as our mini-online daily newspaper."

Created in one day by the in-house marketing media group, the blog allows readers to access an archive of posts dating back to March 2006 and lets readers print posts or e-mail a link to the blog to a friend or colleague.

Any public relations staff member can post information on the news blog.

"The flexible and casual design of a blog gives us the freedom to publicize a greater variety of events and news about community members than we would be able to by using more traditional methods," says Chmura.

He says that so far the response to the blog has been extremely positive and reporters are using it as a resource for story ideas.

When it comes to formatting a news blog, the options vary from posting brief updates as frequently as several times a day to posting lengthy updates less often.

"My personal preference is to post brief items on a regular basis," Chmura says. "Images, photos, logos, even clip art all help to brighten up the presentation. It is also important to offer your readers RSS feeds."

Check out the blog at: www3.babson.edu/Newsroom/blog/default.cfm

Source: Michael Chmura, Director of Public Relations, Babson College, Babson Park, MA. Phone (781) 239-4549.

73 Release Inner Child to Lighten Up Website

Looking for easy ways to make your website more lively and fun? The following suggestions will make that challenge seem like child's play:

☐ Use childhood photos of staff members instead of boring or stuffy formal head shots.

☐ Have a "getting to know you" section where staff can each answer five short questions to create a fun profile. (e.g., what is your favorite childhood memory? What did you want to be when you grew up? What was your favorite birthday, and why?)

☐ If your organization serves children or young people, scatter their artwork, poems or quotes throughout the site.

These steps will not only make your website livelier, they may also make your staff seem more accessible while giving the community at large opportunities to connect with the people you serve.

74 Take Your Fact Sheet Online

Maximize your organization's fact sheet.

An at-a-glance look at your organization, this sheet is typically one page that shares the history, mission and scope of the program and gives basic statistical and financial information.

That same document can be a great online resource for reporters and others looking for a snapshot of the work you do.

Here are some tips and samples for making the most of your fact sheet online:

• **Use all the resources your website offers.** With no concern for printing costs, your online fact sheet can highlight multiple programs, resources and information. Quincy College's (Quincy, MA) online fact sheet (www.quincycollege.edu/qc/about/fact_sheet.htm) includes tuition information, organizational charts and student profile data.

• **Use the website to keep fact sheet information current.** Printed fact sheets are static documents that may be updated once a year or whenever statistical information changes. In contrast, your online fact sheet can be fluid and current. This will appeal to reporters or media outlets that cover multiple stories about your organization and want a fresh angle.

• **Have the formats be compatible.** The website for Yale University (New Haven, CT) describes its online fact sheet (www.yale.edu/oir/factsheet.html) as a statistical summary. The Web page has more than two dozen links to other information on the site. However, the very first link is for a two-page, printer-friendly version of the information.

75 ## Cutting-edge Marketing Tool Brings Awareness

How well are you keeping up with the ever-changing world of marketing on a restricted budget?

Officials at Children's Healthcare of Atlanta (Atlanta, GA) rose to that challenge to boost awareness of its already well-established pediatric cardiac service and overall brand, says Kate Sutton, manager of marketing.

Sutton says that as a marketing department in the field of healthcare — where technology is rapidly progressing — they have to progress as well, despite nonprofit budget constraints.

"Print feels safe, but the Web is flexible and digital media can be multi-purposed," she says. Recognizing this trend, she and her staff developed an interactive CD for external physicians with the dual goal of further increasing awareness of the Children's Sibley Heart Center and driving business to the organization.

"We talk about the cutting-edge technology and state-of-the-art facilities we have available for pediatric patients in all of our printed materials and on the Web, but the CD allows us to actually show all of this in action," says Sutton.

They mailed the CD to their target audience, took it to national physician conferences, used it as a leave-behind piece at a local physician outreach and streamed the video onto the cardiac website.

The CD, originally developed for a physician audience, is educating other important audiences, she says. Foundation staff share it with potential donors, the cardiac team shares it with patient families and the recruitment team takes it to nursing schools and job fairs.

While tracking how many people have viewed the CD isn't feasible, Sutton says the CD is equipped with unique URL links that take viewers to different areas of the hospital's cardiac website.

She says that with 1,200 CDs distributed to date, they can track 465 visits to the cardiac website back to the CD.

Source: Kate Sutton, Manager, Marketing, Children's Healthcare of Atlanta, Atlanta, GA. Phone (404) 785-7579. E-mail: kate.sutton@choa.org

Stay Tech-savvy Without Breaking Bank

Is an interactive CD beyond your capabilities and budget? Take smaller steps to stay in the midst of today's high-tech communication efforts, says Kate Sutton, manager, marketing, Children's Healthcare of Atlanta (Atlanta, GA). The organization is making the most of a recently produced CD by sharing it with a wide range of audiences (see related story at left).

"Just because we don't have bottomless budgets doesn't mean we can't be more futuristic in our planning and implementation," says Sutton. "There are inexpensive initiatives we can use that will provide a better return on investment than other more expensive methods."

If you have an in-house Web team or have the skills yourself, start with some inexpensive Web basics:

✓ Include and regularly update RSS feeds for Web content to keep your brand consistently in front of your audience. "Our PR team put an RSS feed on their media room and it's been a huge success with their target audience," says Sutton.

✓ Add streaming video to make site more interactive.

✓ Create a way for the Web user to provide feedback or contact you with questions (e.g., online forms). "These are user-friendly because the user is already online," she says. "They can fill out the form to request more information or register for an appointment and an e-mail is sent to the project manager for fulfillment."

✓ Send branded blast e-mails to your audience base as a quick, easy way to keep them in the loop.

Content not available in this edition

Web Blog Builds Foundation for Long-term, Online Networking

Three Easy Ways to Keep Up With Your Blog

Jennifer Matrazzo, communications director, Prevent Child Abuse New York-PCANY (Albany, NY), says having a year of blogging for the organization under her belt has increased her effectiveness with the tool. She offers the following tips for making the most out of blogging for a good cause:

1. Do as much in advance as you can. Think ahead and make a schedule of posts.

2. Recruit other voices from your organization to guest author, especially ones with specific insight on topics of regional or national importance.

3. Repurpose newsletter and other content. But don't just copy and paste, Matrazzo warns: "Blogging tends to be more informal than other forms of communication and works best when it elicits interaction."

Online social networking sites continue to provide ways for nonprofits to connect with their supporters and others.

At Prevent Child Abuse New York-PCANY (Albany, NY), for example, Jennifer Matrazzo, communications director, was looking for a way to quickly update and disseminate information. She also wanted a venue for information that does not make it onto the organization's website, because either it is too transient or it does not fit neatly into the site's existing structure.

At the same time, PCANY staff wanted a way to update supporters without the need for supporters to visit the website and were looking to take steps into the Web 2.0 world. This perfect storm of needs led PCANY to start blogging in April 2008.

Since then, the blog has been viewed about 6,100 times, she says, noting that page views generally spike after posts about topics getting a lot of national attention.

Matrazzo says the blog is meeting their needs, although slowly. "We have received very positive feedback. Some of our colleagues follow the blog and a couple of our board members have requested to be guest authors."

The blog has also connected the organization with another blogger who is a survivor of child abuse, Matrazzo says: "She links to our blog and often reposts our entries on her own blog."

Downsides of a blog are minimal, she says. "It can be difficult to keep up with the updates. Also, the potential for interaction is a double-edged sword. It can invite comments that are not helpful and don't contribute to the larger conversation."

Still, she says she believes that ultimately the interactive nature of a blog will be a plus for the organization and their cause as a whole. "Over time, we hope to connect with more followers, like the survivor mentioned above, and build a strong online network of supporters committed to preventing child abuse."

Source: Jennifer Matrazzo, Communications Director, Prevent Child Abuse New York, Albany, NY. Phone (518) 445-1273. E-mail: jmatrazzo@preventchildabuseny.org

 ## Provide Clear Guidelines for Story Submissions

Many organizations allow constituents to submit story ideas via their website. Mercy College (Dobbs Ferry, NY) goes a step further to include nine questions with its online "Submit a Story Idea" form to help users determine if their stories are newsworthy.

"The nine questions that determine news value were included to assist our various constituencies, both internal and external, in better understanding what we look for and how we measure newsworthiness within our department," says Christine Baker, director of public relations. "They are straightforward and help to define the information before it is submitted to our office."

The questions include:

• Does the information have any importance to the prospective reading, listening or viewing public?
• Do you have a new angle on an old story?
• Would the audience pay to know the information?

Baker and her colleagues spend minimal time directing people to the list as most users are familiar with it, she says. "Our internal constituencies really know this information since we have developed relationships with so many faculty and staff already. For our external constituencies, such as alumni and friends, they typically find the newsroom on their own and submit story ideas to us. While we rarely direct external audiences to that page, we know they are finding it because of the story ideas we receive and follow up in our office."

For organizations considering a similar online tool, Baker offers this insight, "As public relations professionals, I think it is important for us to remember that not everyone thinks about those questions before submitting an idea. Further, it helps explain to those who may not know what we do why we request certain information."

Source: Christine Baker, Director of Public Relations, Mercy College, Dobbs Ferry, NY. Phone (914) 674-7596. E-mail: cbaker@mercy.edu

Consider Your Website's Audience Before Making Changes

Before making major changes to your website, think through how doing so may impact your frequent online visitors, especially those who may not be computer savvy.

For example, if many of your supporters are 65 or older, have you researched to determine the best elements to make Web browsing simple for this target audience?

Aaron Howard, senior Web designer at IlluminAge (Seattle, WA), a communications firm specializing in needs of organizations that serve older adults and caregivers, says that when evaluating a website's effectiveness as a tool for reaching older adults, ask:

Are your site's organization and navigation clear? Can users readily tell what's on the site by looking at the home page? If they go to another page, can they figure out how to get back home? To ease navigation, use consistent layout and symbols, and locate top-level navigation buttons in the same place on each page.

Is type readable? Use a sans serif font, no smaller than 10 point. Remember, dark type on a white background is easiest to see. Double-space and left-justify body text. If possible, allow users the option to adjust type size.

Are links and other navigation signals clear? Text with links should be underlined and in a contrasting color. Visited links should then change to a third color. Never underline non-linked text.

Are interface elements suitable for older users? Links and buttons should provide a forgivingly large target for users whose level of manual dexterity doesn't allow them to zero in on precise spots.

Is text designed with senior readers in mind? Shorter paragraphs, few complex sentences and plenty of subheadings and other visual cues help readers process the information. In writing for the Web, less really is more.

Source: Aaron Howard, Senior Web Designer, IlluminAge, Seattle, WA. Phone (800) 448-5213. E-mail: aaron@illuminage.com

Website Elements to Avoid

Make your website simple to navigate, especially for visitors 65 and older or with visual impairments.

According to Aaron Howard, senior Web designer, IlluminAge (Seattle, WA), "many of the bells and whistles that Web developers love can actually hinder the ability of older adults to navigate and comprehend your site."

To keep your website accessible to more people, he says, avoid:

- **Elaborate fly-out menus.** These require precise, coordinated mouse clicks that can be a nightmare for people with arthritis or tremors.
- **Fashionable patterned backgrounds.** These can make text unreadable for older eyes.
- **Large video downloads.** These files can often bring older model computers to a grinding halt.

 ## Spice Up Your Site With Multimedia

Looking for a new way to showcase your organization and grab the media's attention at the same time? Consider adding a multimedia section to your website.

"Our multimedia section of our website aims to capture the essence of cosmetic dentistry in action," says Eric Nelson, director of public relations, American Academy of Cosmetic Dentistry (AACD) of Madison, WI. "In addition, placing video clips of popular programs and news channels helps pique the interest of other reporters and researchers. And, with the online video phenomenon (e.g., Youtube.com) taking hold, it only makes sense to showcase your organization in video whenever possible."

When determining which video clips to include in your multimedia section, Nelson says it's important to identify your organization's specific target audience. For AACD, Nelson says they identified three groups: dental professionals, the public and the media. Nelson says once they were able to focus on a

specific audience they began the search for compelling videos that would grab the community and media's attention. "First and foremost, we wanted to look for video clips that were engaging. Something that pops on camera, like technology," says Nelson.

Nelson says the organization's multimedia section featured video clips that were produced professionally and internally. For example, the Health Forum's Cosmetic Dentistry in Action and in the Accreditation video was professionally produced for about $20,000. The fee also covered airtime and all rights for future use. Clips submitted by doctors and from actual TV broadcasts were used to produce internal videos. In both cases, the video was converted using Windows Media Format so it would be viewable by most Internet users.

Source: Eric Nelson, Director of Public Relations, American Academy of Cosmetic Dentistry, Madison, WI. Phone (800) 543-9220. E-mail: ericn@aacd.com. Website: www.aacd.com

80 Use Website Platform for Ongoing Economic Discussion

When staff at Colby College (Waterville, ME) realized that the economic disruption in financial markets was not likely to be short-lived, they also realized the need to communicate the impact the economy was having on the college — sooner rather than later — says David Eaton, director of communications and marketing.

"Even as we worked to fully understand the economic challenges we would face into the future," Eaton says, "it was clear that we needed to communicate, as fully as we could, information about Colby's financial situation with our internal and external constituencies."

Fortunately from the communications standpoint, Eaton says, Colby President William D. Adams had chosen to focus the majority of his semi-annual State of the College address on the college's finances.

"It was really the first time President Adams publicly discussed the effect of the economic disruption on Colby," says Eaton. "And it was clear that many more people — on campus and off — would be interested in hearing what he had to say."

Within a day of the event, communications staff posted a video of the speech, the audience Q&A that followed it and a transcript of the speech on the president's page at www.colby.edu and linked to it from Colby's home page.

From there, the office of communications built "Colby and the Economy," a Web page focused solely on the financial challenges the college faces. The page features State of the College material, additional multimedia content relevant to the topic and frequently asked questions.

Eaton says they add content at appropriate times (e.g., year-end financial update in mid-December; summary of several on-campus forums held following the January board of trustees meeting, etc.).

Eaton says their intention is to continue using the "Colby and the Economy" Web page as one aspect of a multi-faceted effort to keep Colby's constituencies updated on progress in dealing with the financial challenges the college faces.

Check it out at: www.colby.edu/news_events/colby-responds-to-the-global-financial-crisis.cfm

Source: David Eaton, Director of Communications and Marketing, Colby College, Waterville, ME. Phone (207) 859-4356. E-mail: dteaton@colby.edu

81 Virtual Tour Provides Answer to Communication Challenge

Staff with North Texas Food Bank (Dallas, TX) had a challenge: to get people to realize they weren't a cozy little food pantry, but a major distribution center helping thousands of people.

The solution: a virtual tour on the food bank's website that would tell a story about the organization's day-to-day realities.

Colleen Townsley Brinkmann, chief marketing officer, says that after seeing a virtual tour on another website, she thought the tool could help them overcome the misconception most people had about the food bank.

Enter Ryan Iltis, owner, Green Grass Studios (Dallas, TX), who offered to create a virtual tour and underwrite any expenses.

Iltis and his team shot footage in one day, created the virtual video in two days and developed a virtual tour that shows the food bank's facilities, including the community kitchen and distribution center.

Iltis shares how the virtual tour came together:

- Food bank staff were put in charge of making sure the warehouse was staged and full of food to tell the most compelling story.

- Areas that would make the greatest impact were selected to be photographed.

- Iltis and his team arrived for the one-day shoot to capture the video.

- They color-corrected and stitched footage together to create the virtual tour.

- The virtual tour was uploaded to the organization's website.

Brinkmann says launching the virtual tour in mid-2007 has given the organization an inexpensive way to communicate its message to the average 50,000 users who visit the site monthly and, most importantly, "gives people a much more realistic view of what we do."

View the online tour at:
http://www.ntfb.org/au_virtual_tour.cfm

Sources: Colleen Townsley Brinkmann, Chief Marketing Officer, North Texas Food Bank, Dallas, TX. Phone (214) 347-9594. E-mail: colleen@ntfb.org Ryan Iltis, Owner, Green Grass Studios, Dallas, TX. Phone (214) 880-0101. E-mail: riltis@greengrassstudios.com

> ### Choosing a Firm to Create Your Virtual Tour
>
> When hiring a firm to create a virtual tour, ask these questions, says Ryan Iltis, owner, Green Grass Studios (Dallas, TX):
>
> 1. Do you have Web experience?
>
> 2. Do you have experience stitching and creating 360-degree panoramic photography?
>
> He says average cost to create a virtual tour is $1,500 to $3,500.

82) Promote Employee Experts

Touting employee experts with the media is a great way to bring recognition to your staff and to your organization as a whole. Employee experts can serve as a knowledgeable media resource.

Centre College (Danville, KY) has showcased employee experts for the past 10 years, says Mike Norris, director of communications. Their experts have been featured in numerous high-profile publications, including: USA Today, The Wall Street Journal, Washington Post and the Chicago Tribune.

The communications staff created a special website page dedicated to employee experts. It features about 50 people, listing their contact information, photo and area of expertise, as well as some of their past media coverage. Listing internal experts on your website increases their media and community exposure.

It is important to bring employee experts on board before touting them to the media. For example, Norris recommends that you first ask staff if you can profile them on your website.

The college also promotes employee experts through ProfNet, an online community that connects reporters with expert sources. ProfNet allows you to receive e-mailed inquiries from reporters seeking experts in a certain area, thus providing an opportunity to respond with detailed information about your in-house experts. Centre College began using ProfNet several years ago. While there is an annual fee, Norris feels it is worth the expense, as it has been instrumental in garnering recognition for employee experts.

ProfNet is a great resource, but it can also be challenging. Depending on the number of inquiries you receive, reading through all e-mails and referring reporters to the appropriate expert can be a time-consuming task. However, the process is quicker if you are well-acquainted with experts on your staff.

The benefits of showcasing employee experts include a great morale boost for employees when they receive media interest in their research and added credibility for student recruitment when Centre College professors are featured in regional and national media.

Source: Mike Norris Director of Communications, Centre College, Danville, KY. Phone (859) 238-5718. E-mail: norris@centre.edu

83) Use Website to Document Sustainability Efforts

Creating a Web presence to highlight your organization's sustainability efforts will keep your community informed and allow you to catalog your efforts.

Rowan University (Glassboro, NJ) and Rice University (Houston, TX) have websites dedicated to their respective institutions' efforts to leave a smaller carbon footprint on the environment.

Richard Johnson, director of sustainability at Rice, launched its sustainability site (http://sustainability.rice.edu) in 2005. "These days," he says, "most people look to Web-based sources first when they have questions. I felt it was critical for us to develop a Web presence to communicate what we're doing."

Johnson reviewed other universities' sustainability websites, selecting features and topics he felt were most successful and would be appropriate for Rice. He says a feature that has been especially well-received is the Publicity page. Clicking on the publicity link "makes it easy for outside people to know what's being written about Rice's program, and I find that I constantly refer to that Publicity page to find individual news stories," says Johnson. "Also, the page functions like a timeline, so it's a living history of our sustainability program."

When designing a website, look for ways to drive traffic to your site.

"The challenge for nonprofits is creating traffic to their sites," says Joe Cardona, director of media and public relations at Rowan. "That may mean offering regular tips, creating an e-newsletter that offers valuable resources or being a well-known clearinghouse of information."

Cardona, whose organization's website is www.rowan.edu/rugreen/, recommends asking if your organization is involved in enough green initiatives to warrant the creation of a website dedicated to your efforts.

"Can you keep it fresh?" he asks, noting that people will stop visiting a site if they believe it offers outdated information.

Sources: Joe Cardona, Director of Media and Public Relations, Rowan University, Glassboro, NJ. Phone (856) 256-4236. Website: www.rowan.edu/rugreen Richard R. Johnson, Director of Sustainability, Facilities Engineering and Planning, Rice University, Houston, TX. Phone (713) 348-5003. Website: http://sustainability.rice.edu

Ask Yourself: 'Is an E-zine Right for Our Nonprofit?'

Have you considered creating an e-zine, an online magazine, to distribute information to your constituents?

Mays Business School at Texas A&M University (College Station, TX) introduced an e-zine in 2001 to keep former students and friends of Mays updated on the people and programs at the business school. The e-zine contains feature stories, news briefs, a calendar of events and a perspectives piece submitted by a contributing writer.

Pam Wiley, communications officer, says if your organization is contemplating the addition of an e-zine to your website, there are nine steps to follow:

1. **Determine the goals of your magazine.** Ask yourself: "How will we determine success?"

2. **Conduct research into whether your audience will read an online magazine.** "It doesn't have to be expensive research, but usually every nonprofit has some base audience to determine interest in an e-zine," Wiley says.

3. **Determine the production schedule (e.g., will it be published monthly or quarterly).** "It doesn't have to be monthly but probably a minimum of once a quarter, otherwise it is just information on the Web that changes occasionally."

4. **Answer the question: "What stories will be written and what sections will be featured?"** "If you can't fill up a year's calendar with some sense of what will be written, a magazine may not be a viable option," says Wiley.

5. **Determine who will design, build and maintain the website.**

6. **Determine who will write the stories.** Good stories require time to develop, write and rewrite. "It isn't something to tack onto an already 40-hour-a-week job," says Wiley.

7. **Who will host the website?** Determine if the host will be your organization's Internet provider or webmaster.

8. **Determine how you will notify readers that your e-zine is online or that the latest edition is available.** It cannot be a one-shot notice. People must be notified in some fashion that the latest edition is available.

9. **Meet with the writer(s) and webmaster to discuss the magazine's goals and vision and set up a production schedule with deadlines.** Make sure the final decision maker is at this meeting.

Source: Pam Wiley, Communications Officer, Mays Business School, Texas A&M University, College Station, TX. Phone (979) 845-0193. E-mail: psw@tamu.edu

---

E-zine Pros and Cons

Pam Wiley, communications officer, Mays Business School, Texas A&M University (College Station, TX), identifies the following benefits and pitfalls of implementing an e-zine.

"An e-zine is cost-effective when you have a lot of information, news or stories that can be produced to reach your target audience," says Wiley. Benefits of an e-zine include: the information is online; constituents and the public are able to gain access from anywhere; there are no printing or mailing costs; you have the ability to promote the organization worldwide; and mistakes in stories can be corrected immediately.

While e-zines are cost-effective and offer many advantages to an organization, Wiley says there are also pitfalls. They include: a constant need to develop information; must be refreshed at regular intervals and you must promote the e-zine. "Just because something is on the Web doesn't mean your target audience knows about it," she says.

 Create a Press Room Despite Lack of Media Coverage

While you're building a portfolio to showcase stories about your organization in a press room or media section on your website, there are things you can do to fill empty space.

By placing dynamic stories related to your cause in this section, you will pique the community's and the media's curiosity while building your own portfolio. Here are things you can do to generate buzz and fill space while you're working to gain coverage:

1. Link news stories from other organizations that share a similar message.

2. Write letters to the editors of local publications. If they print your letter, that's one more thing to add to your press room.

3. Write and post press releases written by staff on issues you feel are important to your organization. If you don't have many written materials, post pictures of staff at local events or conferences.

4. Interview community members and local officials and post a written transcript or video of the interview in your press room.

86 Making E-mail Press Releases Work for You

In a time when the Internet and e-mail make it so easy to get news out to the media, it's more important than ever to make sure your news actually gets broadcast or published. To help guarantee your news releases get used:

1. Send e-mail releases only to those news organizations with whom you have existing relationships. List brokers don't always confirm with editors before including them on e-mail lists. Editors unfamiliar with you may view your e-mail release as spam, guaranteeing your news will never see the light of day.

2. Target the release to the right person in the right department. Identify editors and reporters who would be most interested in what you have to say.

3. Send only one release to one person per news outlet.

4. Be sure the people you are sending the release to accept press releases via e-mail. Some editors and outlets still prefer to receive press releases via fax or regular mail. If so, you will need to factor this into your planning time.

5. Show that you respect the time of editors and reporters by keeping your releases brief. If they require more information, they will ask.

Source: PR Fuel, eReleases.com, Kingsville, MD. Phone (410) 679-1792. Website: www.ereleases.com/pr/prfuel.html

87 Online Cards Can Serve as a Valuable Campaign Resource

Cards sent by e-mail — e-cards — can encourage donations while also thanking donors for their contributions.

Staff with the Westmoreland County Food Bank (Delmont, PA) used two e-card designs for a Thanksgiving 2007 campaign that asked supporters to donate the cost of one or more turkeys for families in need. Both e-cards featured an image of a turkey along with text asking for a donation, says Deana Pastor, Web and program director.

"If the constituent clicked on the Make A Difference link, they were directed to a donation form. Each level of the donation had a label like Buy 1 Turkey, Buy 2 Turkeys, etc.," Pastor says. "After the donation was made, they were given the option to send an e-card mentioning their donation and encouraging others to do so."

They sent the original e-card to the food bank's entire database (1,344 people) and received 49 donations totaling $3,400 from that campaign, says Pastor. The second e-card, which appeared on the online thank-you page, was forwarded on 21 times.

While some organizations may have the software and staff/volunteer talent to create e-cards in house, Pastor says her organization used an Internet software and services company called Convio (www.convio.com), which had also been charged with the food bank's website redesign.

While cost for producing e-cards varies depending on factors such as whether you need to solicit design from an outside company and whether an e-card design is part of a larger project, Pastor says the online tools provide a convenient and notable way to send a message to your supporters.

"I think e-cards are great on many levels," she says. "First, it's a good way to garner support. Someone donates, tells their friends and family, and then even if they don't donate, they are aware of the food bank. That's the hardest challenge for any nonprofit — getting your name out there, and making the public aware of what you do and the struggles you have."

"E-cards are also visually appealing," Pastor adds. "Instead of having tons of text that people most likely won't read, you have an eye-catching image and just a small tag line that hopefully makes people want to help."

Source: Deana Pastor, Web and Program Director, Westmoreland County Food Bank, Delmont, PA. Phone (724) 468-8660, ext. 29. E-mail: deana@westmorelandfoodbank.org

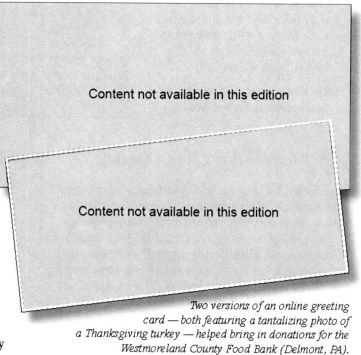

Content not available in this edition

Content not available in this edition

Two versions of an online greeting card — both featuring a tantalizing photo of a Thanksgiving turkey — helped bring in donations for the Westmoreland County Food Bank (Delmont, PA).

Keep Your Media List Up to Date

Changes in staff, duties and priorities on the part of media outlets can make your job of keeping an up-to-date media list time consuming and costly. However, there are low-cost and no-cost ways to ensure that your media list stays current.

Rebecca Wilkowski, director of communications, American College of Traditional Chinese Medicine (San Francisco, CA), oversees a media list of roughly 1,300 contacts. One method she uses to keep contacts current is to include a message in her e-mail signature asking them to let her know if they are not the appropriate contact for the information or inquiry she is sending. The message states:

"If you are not a member of the media, and would like to be removed from this recipient list, please reply to this e-mail with the word 'remove' in the subject line. If you are no longer the correct point of contact for your media outlet, we appreciate you letting us know. Thank you!"

"Media contacts change often," Wilkowski says. "Including this note is part of our consistent effort to keep our list updated."

The communications director also pays close attention to e-mails sent back as undeliverable and uses this information to update her media list. She checks for the error code included in the e-mail to see if the user no longer exists or if the recipient's mailbox is simply full. If the user is no longer valid, the contact is removed from the list.

The most time-consuming method the communications director uses to update the college's media contact list is twice-yearly phone calls to every contact on the list. Before making the calls, Wilkowski often visits the media outlets' websites to look for updated contact information.

While she usually makes the calls herself, she does occasionally have the help of a student. Calls are made every six months and can take anywhere from a few days to a month depending on how many calls are made each day. "It is time consuming, but much more reliable than hoping the reporters will update me," says Wilkowski.

While calling or e-mailing each contact may seem overwhelming, doing so may sometimes be the most effective way to get a response.

In addition to reaching out to your media contacts individually, she says, use every opportunity you can to send a message to many contacts at once. For example, include a message in your online press room that asks media contacts to follow up with you when they have a staff change in their office. Also, include a card in your printed media kits reminding outlets to update your office when they have staff changes so that you can ensure you are contacting the right person with future story ideas.

Source: Rebecca Wilkowski, Director of Communications, American College of Traditional Chinese Medicine, San Francisco, CA. Phone (415) 355-1601, ext. 12. E-mail: RebeccaWilkowski@actcm.edu

 ## Blogs Brings Student Voices to the Recruitment Process

Imagine being able to follow the lives of several students for a whole year, for an up-close and personal look at what a college is really like, before deciding whether you want to go there.

That's what staff at Bucknell University (Lewisburg, PA) created with A Year in the Life blogs (http://yearinthelife.blogs.bucknell.edu).

Molly O'Brien-Foelsch, senior writer, says the concept started in 2004. Initial versions chronicled lives of first-year students who posted written entries and photos in eight themed issues a year.

Today, A Year in the Life has been converted into a standard blog. The themes have been eliminated and students blog on topics of their choosing.

University staff, faculty members and student interns recommend students whom they think would be great bloggers. Those candidates then complete an application and selection process.

Bloggers are expected to post at least once a week. They are provided with a list of topics from which to choose, if they wish, but are encouraged to write about anything on their minds as long as the material is appropriate and relevant to Bucknell's prospective student audience.

Blogger posts are pending until approved by O'Brien-Foelsch, who reviews them with as light a touch as possible.

"The bloggers are great admissions recruiters," she says. "They know their audience, and their enthusiasm for Bucknell is clear."

Bloggers get to highlight their writing and photography abilities, while demonstrating to prospective employers or graduate schools that they are well-rounded, highly engaged and community-oriented.

How does Bucknell benefit from the student blogs?

"The blogs help prospective students get a feel for the culture of the place, the personalities of the students and the possibilities available to them," says O'Brien-Foelsch. "The project is intended to reach the kind of prospective students Bucknell wants to recruit — those who are passionate about academics and want to have personal connections with their professors."

Source: Molly O'Brien-Foelsch, Senior Writer, Bucknell University, Lewisburg, PA. Phone (570) 577-3260. E-mail: mobrien@bucknell.edu

90 Highlight Communications Staff Online

Turn the spotlight on your communications staff with a website devoted to your communications department and its services.

At University of California, Davis (Davis, CA), communications staff had developed websites for many campus units, but not for their own department, says Lisa Lapin, assistant vice chancellor, university communications.

"We really are a service unit and we wanted to make it as easy as possible for the many people we work with on and off campus to access the many services we provide and to seek our help," says Lapin. So they created a website dedicated to the communications department (http://ucomm.ucdavis.edu).

The 60-page site — with publication resources, staff bios, contact information for media, internal campus communication guidelines and more — took seven months to create. Web staff spend minimal time keeping it up to date.

Susanne Rockwell, university communications Web editor, says that before the specialized site was launched, "We didn't really have a site that was central to University Communications and nobody knew where to find us."

The website's goal "was to improve service to our constituents by making it easier for them to get information," Rockwell says. "We accomplished our goal of showing service with a personal touch by initiating staff photos and bios and organizing the whole site to allow people easy access to information and service. We also improved index pages for the media and campus community so people could find what they wanted easily — the one-stop shopping idea."

The site was also designed with staff in mind, she says. "We wanted to offer to our internal folks a rational approach to news priorities and communicate guidelines to the campus by posting a matrix with guidelines for news, honors and events publicity. It is amazing how people more easily understand and accept our judgment when we can show them a matrix with a well-thought-out chart of how we measure how to treat various news stories."

For organizations who plan to highlight communications staff online, Rockwell advises, "Get your office involved and explain why having their photos and professional information on the Web is a good thing. Don't make pages that are hard to update. If you have a lot of turnover and problems keeping software programmers, it is tough to update the bio files."

Sources: Susanne Rockwell, University Communications Web Editor; Lisa Lapin, Assistant Vice Chancellor, University Communications, University of California, Davis, Davis, CA. Phone (530) 752-9842.

Content not available in this edition

Content not available in this edition

Providing easy-to-navigate links to key information (top page) and biographies and contact information for staff (above) were two goals that University of California, Davis staff had in mind when they created a website especially to spotlight their communications department.

Communications Website, by the Numbers

Susanne Rockwell, university communications Web editor, University of California, Davis, shares these statistics regarding its website dedicated to the university's communications department:

- 23,326 unique visitors over 12 months looking at 72,000 pages for an average of 2.6 pages per visitor.

- Average of 200 page views a day to this 60-page site.

- About 42 percent of visitors arriving at site via search engine.

- Almost 40 percent of visitors are internal (from within UC Davis).

91 **Facebook Helps Reach Young Alumni**

The newest generation of philanthropists is growing up online, interconnected and savvy about the Internet and technology in myriad ways. To stay vital, nonprofits must incorporate these latest technology tools into their communications vehicles.

Officials with Kimball Union Academy (Meriden, NH) did just that in the summer of 2008 by launching a Facebook page (www.facebook.com/pages/Meriden-NH/Kimball-Union-Academy/15251689582?ref=ts).

Julia Brennan, director of communications and one of three staff members who promote and manage the page, says since the launch they have gained 467 fans (10 percent of alumni).

"Although we haven't fully implemented our plan to promote the page, we anticipated the launch of the Facebook page would be a powerful vehicle for connecting with young alumni, and the demographics reflect this," she says.

Through an Insights feature in Facebook, organizations can obtain data about fans' profiles. Fans in the 18 to 24 and 25 to 34 age groups have been the largest groups to visit the organization's page at 39 and 27 percent, respectively.

"We chose to launch the Facebook page because we felt we were losing contact with young alums at various junctures in their lives, particularly as they went off to college, and then again when they left college," says Brennan. "This is one prong of a concerted effort to stay in touch with them electronically."

The Facebook page includes features such as school fun facts, a blog-style insider discussion and an RSS link to the organization's website news page.

Source: Julia Brennan, Director of Communications, Kimball Union Academy, Meriden, NH. Phone (603) 469-2332. E-mail: jbrennan@kua.org

Considering a Facebook Page?

Wonder if a Facebook page is right for your organization? Here are some advantages of such a Web page compared to a user profile:

✓ Facebook pages are visible to everyone online, even people not logged in to Facebook. A user profile can only be seen by the user's friends and others in their networks.

✓ Facebook pages can have an unlimited number of fans. Regular users can have up to 5,000 friends.

✓ Users can automatically support an organization's Facebook page without confirmation. User profiles must approve incoming friend requests.

✓ Facebook lets you send updates to all your friends. User profiles cannot message all their friends at once.

One downside to a Facebook page is that you will be unable to access your fan's personal contact information.

Seven Tips for Launching Your Nonprofit's Facebook Page

To create a Facebook page while making sure it's a hit with your fans:

1. **Create a free user profile.** Go to facebook.com and click sign up. You'll fill out basic information, receive a confirmation e-mail and click the link in the e-mail. You now have a user profile.

2. **To create a Facebook page, go to www.facebook.com/pages/create.php.** Type the name of the page exactly as you want it to appear and as you think users will search for it. Remember, you won't be able to change the name later.

3. **Select the category of your organization,** for example, a school would select education.

4. **Add content and publish your page.** Choose information that showcases your staff, donors and volunteers. Remember, the stronger the page you create, the more of an effect it has on viewers.

5. **Update your page frequently.** The more often you add new content, the more often people will come back to your page. You can also send updates to your fans to announce news and events.

6. **Harness the power of news feeds.** News feeds on user home pages tell them what their friends are doing. When a user becomes your fan, the news feed feature tells their friends and invites them to become fans, too, which can lead to alumni and friends connecting to your nonprofit.

7. **Choose the application best for you.** While your page comes installed with basic applications, you can build your own applications that are more useful to your constituents.

92 Preview New Website Design Before Launch

Before launching your new website, hold a preview period for staff and constituents. Doing so will allow you to garner valuable feedback and make necessary changes before your big reveal of your new site.

Staff at Temple University (Philadelphia, PA) launched its new website in 2008, three weeks after a week-long preview by administrators, faculty and staff.

The preview, which allowed users to view the new home page and more than two dozen first-level pages, brought in some 200 responses.

Preview Seeks Feedback, Validation of Persons Being Surveyed

The goal of the preview was two-fold, says Mary Beth Kurilko, director of Web communications: to gain valuable information that could be used in the redesign and to let the internal audience know that their opinions were valued.

Planners brought the redesigned website to the university president for approval first, and then to a council of deans before making it available for other internal audiences.

They also sent a survey to faculty and staff before the preview began to find out what they liked about the old website and what they would like to see in the new site. This survey resulted in close to 1,000 responses and was helpful during the design period, she says.

Kurilko says university staff felt it was important to obtain the opinions of the internal audience and let them know what to expect from the new site. Faculty and staff were sent an e-mail asking them to visit the current home page for a link to the preview.

Survey Combines Outside Firm's Expertise, Internal Database

The university utilized an outside design firm to create the concepts for the new site. An internal computer services team handled the preview, including the database used to input feedback and creation of the feedback form. Those participating in the preview were given the option of e-mailing their thoughts or using the feedback form. The form asked for the name, e-mail address and subject, and included a box to type in their comments.

In creating the feedback form, Kurilko notes, "We wanted the form to be something simple that could live on the site once it went live."

Survey Brings Useful Feedback, Results in Pre-launch Changes

Kurilko says the preview survey was well worth the effort. While no major design changes were made due to the preview feedback, she says, many small changes were made as a result.

For instance, some visitors pointed out missing links and other glitches that were updated before the launch.

While university staff conducted the formal preview period over one week's time, the feedback form remains available online and allows students and faculty to continue to send responses, should they have comments or suggestions regarding the website.

For organizations considering making their new site available for a preview period, Kurilko recommends getting buy-in from your president or executive director beforehand.

Source: Mary Beth Kurilko, Director of Web Communications, Temple University, Philadelphia, PA. Phone (215) 204-4332. Website: www.temple.edu

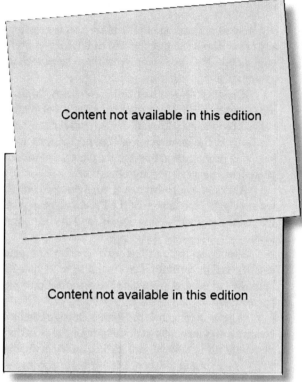

Content not available in this edition

Content not available in this edition

Feedback from faculty and staff prior to online launching of a new website design helped communications staff at Temple University (Philadelphia, PA) implement effective changes. At top is the new design; below it, the old design.

Survey Relies on Online Tools

When staff at Temple University (Philadelphia, PA) sought feedback about a proposed website design, they turned to Zoomerang (www.zoomerang.com), an online survey tool.

Mary Beth Kurilko, director of Web communications, says her office created the survey with Zoomerang's help to solicit feedback from faculty and staff. Zoomerang offers nonprofits a discount on their services, $149 for one year.

The survey consisted of eight questions asking users to rate the website pre-makeover. Questions sought input on the website's look and feel, navigation and search features.

Other questions included:

• What do you like/dislike about the website?
• What are your recommendations for the new site?

All survey participants had the option to enter a contest to win an 80GB video iPod upon submitting their survey results.

Do-it-yourselfer Can Create Cost-effective Podcasts

The cost of developing a podcast for your nonprofit holds the same basic rule of thumb as anything else — simplicity equals value.

Lisa Wehr, CEO, Oneupweb (Lake Leelanau, MI), says the cost of creating a podcast can range from $100 to $5,000, depending on the kind of broadcast.

"Podcasting can be very inexpensive at the lowest quality levels for a very low-budget do-it-yourselfer," says Wehr.

If your nonprofit uses Macintosh computers, the software is already in place for podcasting. If not, software will cost $80 to $100. Wehr notes that it is important to remember server space must also be purchased. Depending on your bandwidth usage, some server space can cost $10 per month.

"The downside of all this is it is a lot of work. You need to come up with the content, write the script, produce the show, edit the files, design the cover art, ready the files for RSS distribution, distribute the files to the directories, optimize the podcast so they show up in the search engines and so forth."

It may be easier to use a professional. Companies such as Oneupweb produce podcasts for a minimum of $5,000. Their services include: search engine optimization of your podcast; research; scriptwriting; cover graphics; landing page design; voice talent; recording; editing and distribution.

Source: Lisa Wehr, CEO, Oneupweb, Lake Leelanau, MI. Phone (231) 256-9811. E-mail: info@oneupweb.com

 ## Use E-mail Signatures to Spark Conversation

Many nonprofit professionals use e-mail signatures for much more than basic contact information, using them to promote special events and campaigns.

Why not take this practice a step further and use e-mail signatures to inspire and spark conversation?

Kasandra Gunter Robinson, senior director of marketing/PR, Capital Area Food Bank (Washington, DC), regularly includes a quote in her e-mail signature. Her current favorite comes from Nelson Mandela, "Where poverty exists, there is not true freedom."

Food bank staff are allowed to choose their own quotes to share in their e-mail signatures, Robinson says. "I like quotes that might stimulate conversation or spark thought," she says. "I've gotten comments on many of the quotes I have included in my signature."

Robinson shares a couple of the favorite quotes she has used in e-mail signatures:

- "I have the audacity to believe that people everywhere can have three meals a day for their bodies, education and culture for their minds, and dignity, quality and freedom for their spirits." — Martin Luther King, Jr.

- "Food means so much more than nourishment. It is what binds us together as families, as communities and as human beings." — Marcus Samuelsson, chef at New York's restaurant Aquavit.

Robinson's favorite sources for quotes are www.quoteland.com and www.quoteworld.org, as well as the food bank's guest speakers. She recommends creating a list of thought-provoking quotes that you can pull from over time.

> **Seek Signature Quotes**
>
> Here are a few examples of websites that provide free quote searches:
> - www.quotationspage.com
> - www.brainyquote.com
> - www.quotegarden.com
> - www.great-quotes.com

Source: Kasandra Gunter Robinson, Senior Director of Marketing/PR, Capital Area Food Bank, Washington, DC. Phone (202) 526-5344, ext.225. E-mail: robinsonk@cfoodbank.org

 ## Hospital Website Connects Patients and Loved Ones

Look for unusual, unexpected and potentially newsworthy ways to serve your constituents.

For more than five years, Presbyterian Hospital (Albuquerque, NM) has offered patients' families and friends the service of its free online greeting card company.

Whether sending congratulations on a new baby, words of support or a get-well wish, persons simply visit the hospital's website (www.phs.org).

As mainstreet supervisor, Toni Gutierrez checks the e-mail inbox twice a day, Monday through Friday, prints the e-greeting cards and hand-delivers them to patients. Gutierrez says they deliver around 1,100 e-greetings annually, including messages from as far away as Holland and Switzerland.

"This service truly makes our patients happy as they hear from someone who is thinking of them while they are sick, or if they are being congratulated for introducing a new baby into the world," says Gutierrez.

She notes that the messages remain private unless patients request they be read to them.

Source: Toni Gutierrez, Mainstreet Supervisor, Presbyterian Hospital, Albuquerque, NM. Phone (505) 841-1144. E-mail: tgutierre2@phs.org

96 Don't Overwhelm Internal Audiences With Outside Ads

Does your organization receive an overwhelming number of requests to market products and services to internal audiences? Create a policy defining the type of access you allow to establish a consistent process for responding to these inquiries in an efficient manner.

Staff with St. Norbert College (De Pere, WI) include a marketing services policy on the college website stating the college reserves the right to deny distribution of any materials considered not to be in line with their mission.

"The statement on our website was created to help those who wish to market their products or services to our students know that we may not always accommodate their request," says Bridget Krage O'Connor, vice president, enrollment management and communications. "For example, if a company wants to promote its product via our internal broadcast system or utilize our e-mail lists, we most likely will refuse."

O'Connor says her office frequently receives requests from businesses seeking to market products or services to students on campus. Many are looking for direct access to students through the college's internal communication systems, such as e-mail lists and internal newsletters. In these instances, the communications team refers the businesses to the student newspaper, which allows local businesses to purchase advertisements.

While they want to ensure that their students have access to a wide variety of opportunities — including special discounts on services — O'Connor says they also want to ensure students are not inundated with advertisements through school e-mail system and other internal channels. Also, she says, allowing requests to go through unscreened may imply the college endorses a particular product or service, even if that is not so.

The screening process includes one noticeable exception, events and services that have to do with the college's founding entity, the Norbertine Order of Catholic Priests and St. Norbert Abbey (De Pere, WI). The college's communications staff often promotes the order's spiritual programming and events directly to students and alumni.

When implementing such a statement or policy, O'Connor says, be sure to inform all staff of the policy and how to implement it properly.

"There is clarity in what our policy says and does," she says. "It helps us ensure we are consistent across the board in how we handle requests and how we use, or don't use, communications systems as it relates to marketing our students. Students should be able to choose what interests them. Conventional marketing methods to reach students, such as ads in the student newspaper, are more appropriate than us giving access to our contact lists and electronic communication tools."

Source: Bridget Krage O'Connor, Vice President, Enrollment Management and Communications, St. Norbert College, De Pere, WI. Phone (920) 403-3109. E-mail: bridget.oconnor@snc.edu

The marketing services policy of at St. Norbert College (De Pere, WI) is featured prominently on the Office of Communications' website (www.snc.edu/communications/marketing/).

Content not available in this edition

97 Three Ways to Make Your Website More Interactive

Looking for ideas to engage your supporters and get them more involved through your website? Check out the website for Mercy Medical Center (Cedar Rapids, IA) at www.mercycare.org for a virtual treasure trove of ways the medical center's website provides a valuable service to constituents, including:

- **Ask the expert.** Visitors can ask questions of a panel of medical experts from the center. They can also review questions recently asked by other visitors and frequently asked questions, along with the answers to those questions.

- **Send a cheer card.** Want to send a card to a patient at Mercy? Simply visit its website, select a type of card, fill out some basic information (patient name and room number, your name, personal message) and send. You can choose to have the card printed and delivered by the hospital or sent to the patient's e-mail address.

- **Visit a patient online.** Patients can easily create their own Web page via the Mercy Messenger to keep family members and friends updated on their status. A patient can be visited from anywhere via the Internet, plus receive alerts every time his/her patient page is updated.

98 Personalize Screen Savers

Personalized screen savers are a cost-effective, eye-catching way to publicize your organization.

"We began offering downloadable Calvin screen savers in March 2001," says Phil de Haan, director of communications and marketing, Calvin College (Grand Rapids, MI). "The idea was simply to add something fun and entertaining to our website while connecting people with the college."

They used Adobe Flash and FlashForge by Goldshell Digital Media to create the screen savers at minimal cost, says de Haan. While a license for FlashForge was approximately $60 in 2001, he says it is now freeware.

Luke Robinson, Web manager, came up with the idea for the screen savers, which he describes as the next logical step after creating downloadable wallpaper for PC desktops.

He worked with the graphic designer and a student to develop the screen savers. They were created relatively quickly, with the first one taking the most amount of time.

"It took about eight hours of development to find the right screen saver authoring application and develop the website," says Robinson. "The student who created the Flash animation spent about eight hours learning how to create a seamless loop and transitions. Afterward, each new screen saver was a matter of replacing artwork, exporting a new Flash movie and authoring the screen saver in Goldshell."

They used images from several sources, including the campus wall calendar and online photo galleries of campus events and academic pursuits.

To publicize screen savers, officials sent an e-mail to faculty and students via the campus listserv and added a link to the home page of the college website. The screen savers are also used in the computer labs and campus information stations.

Robinson says the most challenging aspect of the project is finding exceptional images. Once such images are identified, he says, let them take center stage, keeping logos and other information minimal.

Sources: Phil de Haan, Director of Communications and Marketing; Luke Robinson, Web Manager; Calvin College, Grand Rapids, MI. Phone (616) 526-6475 (de Haan) or (616) 526-8686 (Robinson).
E-mail: dehp@calvin.edu (de Haan)
or lrobinso@calvin.edu (Robinson)

99 E-publication Pros, Cons

Most nonprofit organizations produce a wide variety of publications, many of which are e-publications that exist only in electronic format.

Sharing their thoughts on the pros and cons of producing e-publications are Warren Bell, associate vice president, university and media relations, and Richard Tucker, director of publications (print and online), at Xavier University of Louisiana (New Orleans, LA):

Positives of E-publications:

- Publishing online makes printing current items easier as you are not faced with time and labor associated with producing hard copy materials, plus there is no lag time for printing and distribution.

- If you make a mistake, it is easily correctable online, whereas in print, the mistake is in stone forever.

- Inexpensive to produce or distribute.

- Speed of delivery — in most cases, gets to where you want in seconds.

- Somewhat easier to lay out than print publications, depending on the form and format you use.

Negatives of E-publications:

- Not everyone can receive e-publications. Believe it or not, not everyone has an e-mail address.

- Even many persons with e-mail addresses don't want additional stuff sent to their e-mail accounts.

- Many people prefer hard copies they can hold in their hands. Case in point: Xavier has a postal mailing list of more than 15,000 alums, and yet, the e-mail list is under 4,000.

- Limited shelf life — Once e-mail newsletter is read, it is most likely deleted by reader, whereas a printed piece might survive for a few months on the family coffee table and/or corporate or foundation lobby.

Sources: Richard L. Tucker, Director of Publications (print & online); Warren A. Bell, Jr., Associate Vice President, University & Media Relations; Xavier University of Louisiana, New Orleans, LA. Phone (504) 486-7411.
Website: www.xula.edu/institutional-advancement/index.php

Web Survey Yields Fast Feedback

Online surveys reach a broad audience while providing quick responses.

At YMCA of Greater Rochester (Rochester, NY), Mary Kay Walrath, vice president, communications, says, "We're asking our website users and visitors to provide us with feedback regarding how they use our website, what they look for when they visit and how we can better present the information they need."

Users link to the survey from the YMCA's homepage. Surveys are designed and maintained in-house with help of Zoomerang (http://info.zoomerang.com).

"Zoomerang is a very inexpensive, user-friendly tool," says Walrath. "Our cost was less than $500 for the year, including unlimited surveys."

Walrath says online surveys are an effective way to obtain fast, easy feedback. "They are easier to use and far less intrusive than traditional snail mail or pen-and-paper surveys. Our response rate for this particular (September 2007) survey was around 25 percent, but we've had response rates of nearly 40 percent with other online surveys."

While the YMCA does not have a database to store survey results, Zoomerang gives the ability to import survey results into an Excel file. It also offers tutorials and templates.

Results of the recent online survey — six questions that took five to 10 minutes — showed the majority of the YMCA's web users seek current program schedules and information, and this information wasn't currently easy to find and/or accurate.

Walrath says they will continue using online surveys, and recommends other nonprofits do so, too. "In fact, if I could phase out paper surveys altogether, I'd do it today! However, we have to keep in mind that we have a number of customers who are not comfortable using the Internet and would therefore be unlikely to participate" in online surveys.

Source: Mary Kay Walrath, Vice President-Communications, YMCA of Greater Rochester, Rochester, NY. Phone (585) 263-3928. Website: www.rochesterymca.org

Sample Online Survey Questions

How often do you visit our website?

Why do you visit our website (e.g., schedules, program registration, to make a donation, etc.)?

Please rate specific areas of our website (e.g., maneuverability, accuracy, attractiveness).

Identify two things you would add to or change about our website.

 ## Use YouTube to Bring Your Message Home

Use the virally popular online video hosting site, YouTube (www.youtube.com), to inspire and educate others about your cause.

When Theresa Petrone, campaign manager-special events, Leukemia & Lymphoma Society (Albany, NY) first saw the video "Jake's Journey" on YouTube, she was so touched by the message that she immediately began sharing it with potential fundraising participants.

The video showed images of one of the honorary patients for the chapter's Man & Woman of the Year campaign before, during and after leukemia treatment.

The reaction was so positive, Petrone asked the mother of the other honorary patient for photos of her child "so I could tell the story of both of these brave children."

Links to the videos appear on the campaign website and fundraising participant recruits also received the link via e-mail. The organization has created its own YouTube channel at: www.youtube.com/user/LeukemiaLymphomaSoc

Petrone offers tips for creating videos about your organization for YouTube:

1. **Assembling videos requires special software.** Seek out someone with the necessary software and technical savvy who is willing to volunteer in exchange for recognition and mention.

2. **Be careful that what you post doesn't violate copyright laws.** Petrone says one of their videos was flagged and subsequently removed because of copyright issues related to the background music they used.

3. **Make videos multi-purpose** to make the investment of your time and effort worthwhile. Petrone says the videos they use will also be used at the campaign's grand finale celebration and may become permanent clips on the organization's website.

Petrone says she plans to continue using YouTube for other society business as a way to quickly, easily and inexpensively — via e-mail link or website posting — send a powerful message to potential donors and volunteers.

Source: Theresa C. Petrone, Campaign Manager-Special Events, Leukemia & Lymphoma Society-Upstate New York and Vermont Chapter, Albany, NY. Phone (518) 438-3583. E-mail: theresa.petrone@lls.org

Online Press Kits Newest Trend in Communications

Officials with The American Academy of Orthopaedic Surgeons (AAOS) of Rosemont, IL, realized an online press kit was the most effective method to sharing important news and updates with the media and public.

"After hearing from our PR and media colleagues and reading in the trade magazines that online press kits were the new trend, we sat down as a department and collectively realized this was an arena that we needed to be leaning towards," says Lauren L. Pearson, media relations specialist. "We worked with our IS department to create the functionality and were up and running towards the early part of 2007."

AAOS' online press kit includes news releases, PowerPoint presentation, biographies, event photos, audio, video, additional resource files (e.g., fact sheets), links to similar resources of interest and the press kit logo.

"It is beneficial to create an online press kit because it pre-packages everything one needs to write a story. As journalists are often time-pressed, AAOS wants to give them a place to get everything needed to get a complete story," says Pearson.

Pearson recommends nonprofits interested in creating an online press kit include:

- News releases, fact sheets, bios
- PowerPoint presentations
- Images (graphic or logo)
- Audio (RMT)
- Video (VNR or b-roll)

Once the online press kit is operational, Pearson recommends reaching out to the media for feedback and working with your organization's IS department to monitor which sections get the most hits.

Source: Lauren L. Pearson, Media Relations Specialist, American Academy of Orthopaedic Surgeons, Rosemont, IL. Phone (847) 384-4031. E-mail: lpearson@aaos.org

 Online Photo Journals Serve as a Valuable Publicity Tool

Creating a photo journal section on your website is an excellent way to document both achievements and the spirit of your organization. It can prove a valuable reference for those who are not familiar with your group.

Frank Griffis, director of marketing, LeTourneau University (Longview, TX), explains, "It is part of our strategic marketing plan to show LeTourneau from the students' point of view, rather than the perspective of the marketing department. It also helps prospective students familiarize themselves with our campus. Photos are taken by student Photo Club members. Captions are written by our staff writer or by students themselves. We post the ones we deem appropriate. Authenticity is the key."

Separate journals can be created for special events, including volunteer efforts and fundraisers. To minimize expenses, reach out to staff members who have experience taking photos and are willing to use their own equipment. If your budget allows, invest in camera equipment to be used strictly for this purpose. "We keep a half dozen inexpensive digital cameras on hand for student use when we have activities/events on campus (at night or weekends)," says Griffis.

The university employs a content management system (CMS) to organize and present photos. "The CMS we use is free and open source. We hired a company to assist with initial training and set-up. The cost was about $100,000 for implementation. Since that time, we only pay for upgrades and also purchased a new server to increase scalability," says Griffis. "If you create a photo journal section, be certain that you can keep it fresh throughout the year."

Source: Frank Griffis, Director of Marketing, LeTourneau University, Longview, TX. Phone (800) 759-8811. E-mail: frankgriffis@letu.edu

 Fast-find Website Links Offer Easy Navigation for All

Looking for a simple and effective way to make sure everyone can find what they need on your website? Pay a visit to the website for Catholic Social Services of Alaska (Anchorage, AK) at http://cssalaska.org.

The left side of every page of the website offers fast-find links, phrased in the form of simply worded questions.

Those questions include:
- ❏ "How can I adopt a baby?"
- ❏ "I am new to this country. Where can I get help?"
- ❏ "Where can I find help if I am a homeless teenager?"
- ❏ "Where do I go to find a safe place for the night?"
- ❏ "How do I donate food?"

The easy-to-find links help people in crisis quickly connect with the exact program and information they need, no matter what their level of computer experience is, by selecting one of the simple questions. Each question leads to a page with information about the agency's programs that meet that need.

Source: Katie Bender, Special Events Manager, Anchorage, AK. Phone (907) 276-5590. E-mail: kbender@ccsalaska.org

105 Entice Audience With Top-notch Virtual Tour

A well-designed online tour can virtually transport persons right onto your campus or in the doors of your nonprofit organization. Providing an online tour that is interactive, informative and unique will entice these visitors to learn even more about your cause.

"We had an online tour for several years, but it was really not interesting and had a great deal of old information," says Mike Richwalsky, assistant director of public affairs, Allegheny College (Meadville, PA). "We knew it was time for a refresh."

For that refresh, "We worked closely with a company called New Perspective in Pittsburgh, PA to create our tour," Richwalsky says. "We gathered the photography, wrote all new copy, and recorded and edited the audio voice-overs."

Larry Lee, associate vice president for finance and planning, led a group of five staff members who worked with New Perspective on the project. Meeting every couple of weeks at first and more often as the project continued, Lee says they were able to see the progress being made in real time through an online tour as part of a special website created by the firm.

The college website offers two versions of the tour: guided and self-guided, says Richwalsky. "We find that the explore yourself (self-guided) option is used more by people returning to the online tour. It allows them to jump to a particular building or description if they want to go back and look at more photos, or watch another video."

The guided version leads visitors through various stops on the campus. Each stop may include a description, photos and a video.

One major requirement of the project was that college staff be able to update it as needed. "New Perspective built us a system that allows that," says Richwalsky. "The system is a series of XML files we can easily update with new photos, videos, text, etc."

The entire project took approximately three months and cost $20,000-plus.

According to Scott Friedhoff, vice president for enrollment and communications, the online tour was viewed more than 24,000 times between January and July 2008.

For nonprofits considering an online tour, Richwalsky advises, "Think about what features you want to include because that is often the biggest thing that drives the cost. If you want 360-degree images and you need to shoot and edit new video, plus new campus photography — all that has a cost and that can really skyrocket if you want to include every kind of technology in your tour."

Check out the online tour at: www.allegheny.edu/tour

Sources: Scott Friedhoff, Vice President for Enrollment and Communications; Mike Richwalsky, Assistant Director of Public Affairs; Larry Lee, Associate Vice President for Finance and Planning; Allegheny College, Meadville, PA. Phone (800) 521-5293.

These images from the online tour for Allegheny College (Meadville, PA) show how the interactive site lets persons choose where to visit on campus, then provides video and photographs with more information on the selected site.

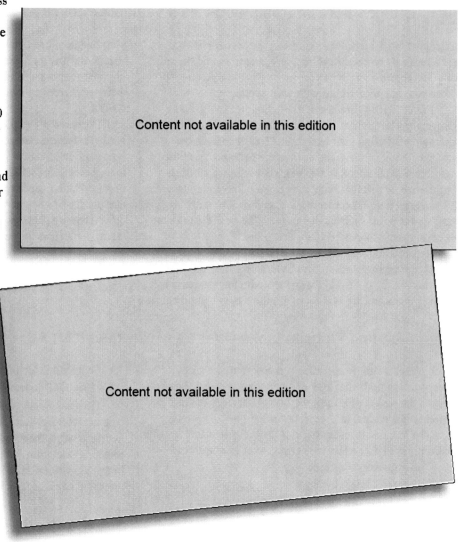

Content not available in this edition

Content not available in this edition

Online Scavenger Hunt Generates Interest for New Website

Last summer, officials with Wayne State University Alumni Association (Detroit, MI) created an online scavenger hunt to garner interest for their redesigned website.

"We completely redesigned the look and navigation of our website, along with a new content management system. We created the scavenger hunt to introduce people to our new site," says Michelle Franzen Martin, director, alumni communications. "The scavenger hunt brought visitors to the home page and motivated them to click through pages they might not otherwise visit."

Martin published a set of 12 questions in the summer issue of the membership magazine, Wayne State Magazine. In order to find the answers, scavenger hunt participants were required to navigate 12 different areas of the website. They mailed or e-mailed their answers to Martin to have their names included in a drawing for five $25 gift cards to the campus Barnes & Noble store. Around 100 people participated in the scavenger hunt.

The alumni association also generated buzz for their new website through Wayne State Magazine advertisements and through e-newsletters.

Source: Michelle Franzen Martin, Director of Alumni Communications, Wayne State University, Detroit, MI. Phone (313) 577-5579. E-mail: michelle.martin@wayne.edu. Website: www.alumni.wayne.edu

 Planning Ahead Helps Spell Success for RSS Feeds

Beth Simpkins, media relations coordinator, Johns Hopkins Medicine (Baltimore, MD), says her department learned the hard way about the importance of thinking through all elements of an RSS feed before — rather than after — creating one.

They created a very basic RSS feed, Simpkins says, "and by the time we realized it was taking off, it was too late to change the URL."

She says she wishes she would have put monitoring mechanisms in place, such as those that track the number of subscribers, who is subscribing using what browsers and where subscribers are located geographically.

A potential downside of RSS feeds is that they may limit your ability to capture visitors' information and reach out to them in other ways, as subscribers may bypass signing up for your e-newsletter or limit their visits to your website.

Knowing these challenges can help you when you begin the planning process. Simpkins advises clearly defining how you see the RSS feeds helping your organization; considering a multi-phase plan for implementing the feed system and evaluating what would be involved in changing the system if there was a need.

Source: Beth Simpkins, Media Relations Coordinator, Johns Hopkins Medicine, Baltimore, MD. Phone (410) 955-4288. E-mail: bsimpkins@jhmi.edu

108 **Highlight Press Releases With a Media Blog**

Create a media relations blog to spotlight press releases and include interactive features.

In September 2007, the media relations team at Lourdes College (Sylvania, OH) launched a media relations blog specifically to post press releases. Written by staff, students and alumni, the blog's goal is to communicate the most current Lourdes news to the public, says Heather Hoffman, media coordinator and chief author of the blog.

"Media has become so interactive that I just don't think the typical press release, all text and no action, packs the same pizzazz that an interactive tool like a blog has," says Hoffman. While they still post press releases in an online newsroom, "I enjoy using the blog to post press releases because it allows others to give feedback and comment on stories. It also offers features that typical attachments do not,"

such as the ability to embed videos, slideshows and photos.

The college's Web content administrator and the director of college relations, in conjunction with Thread Information Design (Maumee, OH), created the blog center that includes the media relations blog and others related to the college.

Response from staff, students, alumni and the community has been positive, says Hoffman, noting that the local media has noticed the releases listed on the blog as well.

For nonprofits considering a media blog, Hoffman offers this advice, "Be as interactive as possible. Post videos, photos and allow for dialogue. This will give your reporting an added touch where a typical press release falls short. Don't be afraid to make your media a dynamic experience!"

Source: Heather Hoffman, Media Coordinator, Lourdes College, Sylvania, OH. Phone (419) 824-3952.

Maximize Your Website's Media-friendliness, Accessibility

Take some simple steps to make your organization's website as user-friendly as possible, especially when it comes to media access. After all, making your website easy to access and maneuver can increase the possibility of getting your story told.

For inspiration, check out these three ways nonprofit organizations who are already putting their websites to use to generate news stories:

- Purdue University (Lafayette, IN) has an Info for Journalists tab on its online event index page (http://news.uns.purdue.edu/eventindex.html). The tab leads to a list of links that can help reporters provide better coverage of the school. The links include a reporters' calendar, listing upcoming events at the school; a story ideas page, with suggestions for ways Purdue faculty and staff can comment on current issues; and an opportunity for media to sign up to receive highly specific news via e-mail. Reporters can choose to be notified immediately whenever a release is sent regarding any number of a very detailed and specific list of topics from each department at the school (e.g., agriculture-soybeans, business-computer technology, science-bubble fusion). This way, reporters are easily able to get only the information they need for their beat.

- Mercy Medical Center (Cedar Rapids, IA) has a media inquiries notice on its Web page (www.mercycare.org/about/news/10th_St.aspx), with instructions how to contact the hospital's media hotline, as well as this text, to let members of the news media know they are welcome to pursue stories:

  We are available to assist members of the news media or the general public with any questions you may have about Mercy Medical Center. Mercy's media relations can also assist with questions about news releases, arrange on-site logistics for visiting news crews and provide background information on the hospital, administration and medical staff.

- Ohio Wesleyan University's (Delaware, OH) website has a news and media page (http://news.owu.edu/) that offers a listing of recent news releases, an expert source guide and a media tips page that shares brief stories about happenings at the university or in the community that impact the university (see related story, below). As the Ohio Wesleyan University Web page says, "There is always something newsworthy happening...." With these tips, you can make sure the media knows what is happening with you!

Website Feature Simplifies Contacts for Media

Looking for a simple way to highlight the expertise of your nonprofit organization's staff, volunteers, board members or clientele? Borrow a page from the website of Ohio Wesleyan University (Delaware, OH).

According to Linda O'Horo, assistant director of media and community relations, the university's communications department experienced a major staff expansion about three years ago and a subsequent increase in media relations efforts. One result of these efforts was the Expert Source listing section on the OWU website (http://news.owu.edu/).

O'Horo says faculty and certain administration staff were recruited to participate. The subject areas and credentials of each expert source are listed. Media are asked to contact one of two media staff to assist in setting up interviews.

O'Horo says the only negative to this feature is ongoing maintenance: "You need to review the listings periodically and edit as needed. It is also important to enlist support or recommendations from department chairs or administration in the recruiting of good expert sources."

Source: Linda O'Horo, Assistant Director of Media and Community Relations, Ohio Wesleyan University, Delaware, OH. Phone (740) 203-6909. E-mail: laohoro@owu.edu

---

 Keep Web Pages Up to Date

Ever visited a website and then clicked on some feature for more information only to be directed to a page that reads The page cannot be found? When that happens, what's that convey? They don't have their act together... they don't give their website the attention it deserves... maybe they're not worthy of my support.

Don't let that happen to your website. Any time you make a change to your website, think what about other changes will be needed. In addition, someone on your staff should regularly visit every website page to confirm that all information is correct and in good working order.

Poll Audiences, Then Choose Social Media

Thinking of creating an organizational presence on a social networking site? Streamline your efforts by first polling your audiences to see which site they prefer, then focusing on the one or two most-popular sites first.

In April 2009, staff with College of the Mainland (Texas City, TX) posted a week-long poll on their home page asking users to choose the online social networking site they used most: Facebook, Flickr, MySpace, Twitter, YouTube or none.

"We wanted to see where we could do some potential advertising and where to reach our students and potential students on the Web," says Lana Pigao, director of marketing and publications. She notes that at the time, the only site the college used was Facebook.

Poll responses were recorded in a database and were analyzed when the college created its annual marketing plan and budget. Staff used the information collected to determine which other social networking options to pursue.

Pigao says the college chose to create an online poll instead of a traditional poll to add an interactive and fun element to their website.

The marketing and communications staff created poll questions, and the college webmaster created the survey in Poll Daddy (www.polldaddy.com), which offers free and paid accounts allowing users to create polls and surveys.

Source: Lana Pigao, Director of Marketing and Publications, College of the Mainland, Texas City, TX. Phone (409) 938-1211, ext. 434. E-mail: lpigao@com.edu

 ## Tips for the New Nonprofit Blogger

So you've got the powers that be on board with starting a Web log, or blog, on behalf of your organization. Now what? The following tips can help you get your blog started and see some return value for your efforts:

❏ **Read other blogs.** This will help you learn what's good, what's not and what people remember. Don't be afraid to reach out to some of your social-media-savvy constituents to see what might interest them in your blog.

❏ **Make sure content is worthwhile and exciting.** If it's not, people will stop caring and will stop coming. Also make sure to have the right person(s) writing it.

❏ **Keep it active.** Come up with a reasonable posting schedule and stick to it. Leaving too much time between posts can lead to people losing interest.

❏ **Keep it informal.** Save the jargon and the formal speak for official publications. Try to write with a more human tone about topics that people care about in words they understand.

❏ **Find ways to get people there.** Your blog might be great, but if no one reads it, who cares? Include a link to your blog as a footer in your e-mails and on your organization's website. Put links to other blogs to drive return traffic. Post comments on other blogs — just make sure they have value for the blog's audience and aren't just a way to get people back to your blog.

Seven Reasons Your Nonprofit Should Blog

Why blog? Because a blog is a quick, easy and free way to get your message out to like minds, people who need your services, prospective donors and volunteers. And that is just for starters.

Here are some additional reasons you might want to consider a blog for your organization:

1. **Blogs are of the moment.** Is there breaking news that affects your organization? Let people know about it instantly.

2. **Blogs are easy to update.** Unlike websites and other more formal Internet fare, blogs can be changed quickly and easily.

3. **Blogs give a voice to others.** By inviting guest bloggers (e.g., board members, donors, volunteers, etc.) you are sharing the importance of the work you do from many different perspectives.

4. **Blogs add transparency to your work.** The timely topics generally covered in blogs give readers a glimpse of the work your organization does daily.

5. **Blogs make your organization human.** Overly branded organizations can take the human right out of human services. Blogs can give that human voice back.

6. **Blogs invite feedback you might not get otherwise.** Looking to test a new brochure or see what people really thought about your last event? Invite comments to your blog and you will be amazed at the insights you receive.

7. **Blogs give you an additional online presence** that can drive people to your website.

Web Tool Connects Patients and Families in Real Time

How would you like to have 15,000 visits to just one page of your website annually for five years, with that same page keeping people connected to your organization long after the official relationship ends?

That is what the Mercy Messenger service online tool (https://www.mercycare.org/patients/messenger.aspx) has done for Mercy Medical Center (Cedar Rapids, IA), says Melissa Erbes, marketing specialist. The tool, custom created for Mercy, keeps patients' friends and families updated on the status of a hospitalized loved one. It has also put Mercy on the national scene, serving as a model for other hospitals across the country.

Here's how it works:

1. Patients set up a custom account complete with name, admission date, room number, phone number and other pertinent information — including whether the patient is accepting calls and visits. Patients can also choose to have a friend or family member manage the account on their behalf. The setup process takes minutes.

2. Next, the individual who set up the account can create a customizable e-mail list to keep everyone up to date.

Friends and family can sign up to receive immediate e-mail alerts each time a new health status posting has been made, or can log in to review the updates at any time. Patients or patient representatives can add new information to the entire list at any time, including health updates and messages. Family members and friends can also send personal get-well greetings.

3. Patients receive a custom patient ID code, allowing them to determine who can access or receive the information.

There is no cost to anyone to use the service. Mercy even has laptops available for their patients and their families to use for free.

Erbes says the response to the online service has been overwhelming and far-reaching. Patients can even continue to use the tool once they are out of the hospital to keep family updated on their health, providing patients with a no-cost, valuable service and providing Mercy with an opportunity to stay top of mind to their constituents.

Source: Melissa Erbes, Marketing Specialist, Mercy Medical Center, Cedar Rapids, IA. Phone (319) 398-6011.
E-mail: merbes@mercycare.org

 ## Share Save-the-date Reminders in Your Publications, Online

Save-the-date cards can be an eye-catching way to promote your upcoming events.

In addition to mailing traditional cards, include save-the-date announcements in print and online publications as a low-cost way to reach a wider audience.

Staff at Providence Hospital (Washington, DC) routinely include such announcements for events put on by The Providence Health Foundation in the hospital's internal newsletter, which has a distribution of 2,880, and external newsletter, which has a distribution of 75,000, says Stephanie Hertzog, director, public relations.

These announcements, coupled with 700 mailed reminders, allow the hospital to reach an extremely large audience at a relatively low cost, Hertzog says. She notes that some of the 700 people included on the direct mail list also receive one of the newsletters, which serve as a second reminder of the upcoming event.

Announcements are designed by a graphic artist who provides the hospital's publications manager with images to be used in both newsletters. Save-the-date announcements included in publications are usually identical to the mailed cards unless they need to be reformatted for print, and are placed in a section highlighting the foundation or on the back cover of the publi-

cation, depending on space.

When using save-the-dates in multiple publications, Hertzog advises keeping the design consistent with postcards or invitations to ensure that persons recognize the information is for the same event.

Source: Stephanie Hertzog, Director, Public Relations, Providence Hospital, Washington, DC. Phone (202) 269-7021.
E-mail: shertzog@provhosp.org

This save-the-date reminder was featured in the Winter 2008 community newsletter for Providence Hospital (Washington, DC).

Content not available in this edition

Web-based Options Help Stop Communication Budget Drain

Whether to save on production costs, speed up dissemination of information or link to your supporters in the trendiest way possible, look for electronic, Web-based options to communicate with your constituency.

Turning to electronic options helped Shelly Grimes rise to a challenge her first day on the job as marketing and public relations coordinator for the Crossroads of America Council of the Boy Scouts of America (Indianapolis, IN), when she learned the organization's leaders felt they were receiving outdated information in their printed newsletters.

That was June 2007. Six months later, the council switched to electronic communications formatting, with the transition project staffed entirely by student volunteers from Indiana University-Purdue University Indianapolis (IUPUI).

The council now produces four versions of its monthly electronic newsletter for various audiences, including volunteers, parents and scouts. Grimes says print is an important component of the overall mix, and the group continues to produce a quarterly print newsletter for recognition and feature stories.

Budget was a secondary — though significant — consideration for transitioning to Web-based communications, Grimes says. "Not only was it a more cost-effective option, but it has served our leaders better. We've gotten overwhelmingly positive feedback," with newsletter subscriptions jumping from 4,000 to 7,600 since launch of the electronic vehicles.

The latest technological tools and toys can boost nonprofits' bottom lines beyond improving communications.

At St. Mary's Food Bank (Phoenix, AZ), for example, a global positioning system (GPS) purchased with grant money is helping organizers plan truck routes more efficiently and cut operating expenses. Program leaders project the collection of more goods without the need for additional trucks and employees, plus savings of $50,000 annually in fuel expenditures.

Sources: Shelly Grimes, Marketing and Public Relations Coordinator, Crossroads of America Council/Boy Scouts of America, Indianapolis, IN. Phone 317-925-1900, ext. 224. E-mail: sgrimes@bsamail.org

---

Postcard Replaces Newsletter In Blog-driven Option

Kivi Leroux Miller (Lexington, NC) president of EcoScribe Communications and Nonprofit Marketing Guide.com, advocates a balanced strategy of online communications and creative print tactics.

For example, in response to some nonprofit leaders lamenting they can only afford to send their print newsletters twice a year, Miller suggests creating full-color postcards, which — at one-third the cost of a four-page color newsletter — can go out six times a year for the same expenditure.

So effective is an attractive postcard, says Miller, that organizations may consider dropping newsletters altogether and augmenting the postcards with informative Web content.

Sources: Kivi Leroux Miller, author, Kivi's Nonprofit Communications Blog, Lexington, NC. Phone (336) 499-5816. E-mail: Kivi@ecoscribe.com. Blog: www.nonprofitmarketingguide.com/blog/category/print-newsletters

---

 ## Drive Traffic to Your Website

What efforts do you make to get people to log on to your organization's website?

The online team for Operation Smile (Norfolk, VA) employs a variety of strategies to drive traffic to the organization's website, says C. Eric Overman, director of online and interactive. Those techniques include DRTV (direct response television), direct mail, e-mail, search engine optimization (SEO), social media, viral marketing, buzz marketing and banner advertising.

Overman says that in the last 24 months, those techniques have helped them enjoy a 50 percent growth in Web traffic, 80 percent growth in online revenue and 500 percent growth in e-mail list size.

He shares tips to help other organizations boost their website traffic:

✓ The most successful campaigns are the ones that are integrated across channels.

✓ Don't just focus on prospects. These techniques can be used to increase engagement with existing donors too.

✓ Use banner advertising to build brand awareness, not necessarily revenue. Overman says, "Banner advertising is tough if you're expecting immediate, positive ROI (return on investment). To work it needs to be very targeted (e.g., directing to a gift in an online catalog)."

Source: C. Eric Overman, Director of Online and Interactive, Operation Smile, Norfolk, VA. Phone (757) 321-3252. E-mail: eoverman@operationsmile.org

Look Online for Low-cost Resources

Finding free and low-cost resources to further communications efforts is valuable to any nonprofit communicator. Many online resources provide valuable services at little to no cost that can help you expand your communications reach.

Katie Crabtree Thomas, director of communications and education, Ohio Psychological Association (Columbus, OH) shares five online resources she and her colleagues use to fulfill their communications needs:

1. **www.shutterfly.com** — "We use Shutterfly to host all of our photos from our events, located at www.ohiopsychologicalassociation.shutterfly.com. It's a good way for all attendees to see photos from our events and it's free to use."

2. **www.istockphoto.com** — With no photography budget for publications, she uses IStockphoto to obtain inexpensive or sometimes free images.

3. **www.i-newswire.com** — "We use I-Newswire to send out news releases. There are two options, $25 per release or a free release that contains advertising from outside companies."

4. **www.helpareporter.com** — Sign up for news tips from journalists looking for sources. A couple e-mails are sent daily for sources, and you can pick and choose which ones apply to you.

5. **www.surveymonkey.com** — "SurveyMonkey allows us to survey our members for a relatively inexpensive price, and it's greener than sending paper surveys." SurveyMonkey tallies results, saving significant staff time.

Source: Katie Crabtree Thomas, Director of Communications and Education, Ohio Psychological Association, Columbus, OH. Phone (614) 224-0034. E-mail: kcrabtree@ohpsych.org

 ## Cater e-newsletter Content to Target Audiences

Q. *How do you target various audiences to get your message out?*

"One way is through e-newsletters. Calvin College (Grand Rapids, MI) has four —Calvin Wire, which offers breaking news and alumni updates; Calvin-Parents (for parents of students); Calvin-Sports Report (featuring the latest on college athletes) and Calvin-Connection, which has information about on-campus programs and events open to the public. This allows us to send our message directly to our constituents, while reaching very distinct audiences. We determined it would be more widely read if the publications were specific to the audience.

"We are also able to inform and remind neighbors and friends about learning opportunities at or sponsored by Calvin and increase attendance at these events, while allowing us to promote photo galleries and video, too.

"Feedback has been mostly positive. We get a lot of thank-yous and many people stay on the lists long after their child has graduated.

"Our distribution frequency varies from twice a month with Calvin Wire to daily for Calvin-Sports Report, with each publication going out to anywhere from 500 (Calvin-Connection) to 6,527 recipients (Calvin-Parents)."

Source: Lynn Rosendale, Associate Director Communications and Marketing, Calvin College, Grand Rapids, MI. Phone (616) 526-6861. E-mail: lrosenda@calvin.edu

 ## Three Unique Benefits of Twitter

Twitter (www.twitter.com) — a free social messaging utility for staying connected in real-time — is just one of the trendy tools nonprofits can use to share their mission.

Mark Armstrong, senior manager, Internet and new media, North Texas Food Bank (Dallas, TX) says Twitter helps them spread their message, supplement fundraising efforts, increase their knowledge base and expand their community of supporters.

He cites additional ways the food bank benefits from the use of Twitter:

✓ **Gathering feedback.** "We have experienced wonderful feedback from Twitter friends while they're on site at our events, such as Empty Bowls and Taste of the NFL."

✓ **Adding transparency.** He says Twitter gives them a unique window to their constituents. "It's a very close two-way street. They can speak their mind and we can deliver our content in a non-threatening way, making the value of our message stronger."

✓ **Driving website traffic.** Including URLs in tweets drives people to your website.

Source: Mark Armstrong, Senior Manager, Internet and New Media, North Texas Food Bank, Dallas, TX. Phone (214) 330-1396. E-mail: mark@ntfb.org

Website Newsroom Tip

Include a Media Room button on your home page that allows the media direct access to downloadable stock photos (print quality of 300 dots per inch).

 ### Website Branding

Keep in mind that each of your website's pages should possess related attributes. Test your Web style consistency by visiting several of your site's pages to identify what's similar about each.

 ### Build Anticipation With Online Countdown Clock

Counting down the days until a major transition or event is a great way to generate excitement among internal and external audiences. Placing an online countdown clock on your website will expose this unique publicity effort to an even wider audience.

In October 2008, Malone College became Malone University (Canton, OH). To mark that milestone, officials posted a countdown clock on the home page of their website. The clock started ticking on May 4, 2008 and counted down the days to the transition, right down to the second.

The countdown clock idea came up in meetings of the transition committee, a group of 20 people charged with planning all events and programs relating to the transition, says Suzanne Thomas, director of university relations. "We saw (the countdown clock) as a way to build excitement while communicating the upcoming change."

The creation of the clock was a collaboration between the university's Web content manager and In The Round (Canton, OH), the firm that handles the design of the university's website. The clock did not require any updating or maintenance on the part of the university.

"We were under a time crunch because our transition team came up with the countdown clock idea and wanted it implemented as soon as possible," says Andrea Finefrock, Malone's Web content manager. "I sat down with In The Round and told them exactly what we wanted; the creative team came up with a mock-up of the clock within two weeks.

"We wanted something that fit within our template of the home page where photos are normally located," and matched existing Web page colors, Finefrock says.

They used the countdown clock along with other publicity efforts and community events designed to create excitement about the name change.

"The countdown clock has proven to be an effective tool used to keep an important event front and center before our publics," says Thomas. "Perhaps the most interesting response came when one of our faculty members was visiting China and a gentleman there said, 'Oh Malone College, only 62 days until you become a university!'"

Finefrock says she has heard from faculty members at other colleges as well as vendors who have taken notice of the clock.

The public relations officials note that a countdown clock could also be utilized to announce other major developments, such as the announcement of a new president, unveiling of a new mascot or the opening of a new building on your campus.

Source: Suzanne Thomas, Director of University Relations; Andrea Finefrock, Web Content Manager; Malone University, Canton, OH. Phone (330) 471-8239 (Thomas) or (330) 471-8514 (Finefrock). E-mail: sthomas@malone.edu

An online countdown clock tracks minutes until Malone College becomes Malone University (Canton, OH).

Content not available in this edition

Survey Readers to Gather Valuable Feedback

Reader surveys can provide valuable feedback that can help shape your publications.

Staff at Salve Regina University (Newport, RI) began using online reader surveys for their Report from Newport magazine in 2003. Originally created as a printed piece that polled alumni for feedback, the survey (www.salve.edu/news/rfn/rfn-survey.cfm) is now posted in the online newsroom of the university's website. The brief survey:

✓ Asks readers to rank in order from one to six a list of topics they would like to see covered in the magazine.

✓ Provides space for readers to fill in other topic ideas in which they are interested.

✓ Solicits general feedback and comments.

✓ Asks alumni to share their news and updates so that their information can be included in the class notes section of the magazine.

The survey is evolving, says Deb Herz, managing editor of publications, university relations and advancement, and developer of the survey questions.

"I'd like to include a section on the survey where readers can write letters to the editor, giving them more of an opportunity to critique the articles and comment on the stories," says Herz. "This would create a forum for feedback and open dialogue, which could lead to editorial improvement."

Developed with help from the university's webmaster, the survey took about a week to create, including drafting the survey, creating and posting the online version. The survey cost nothing beyond staff time to create.

Information submitted through the surveys is stored in the university's database and is used to inspire new topics and features, says Matt Boxler, public information officer, university relations and advancement.

"Submissions for news and events are printed in the magazine and sometimes, after a review from the editorial board, we'll get a larger feature story out of a submission," Boxler says. "One example is a submission received from 1965 Salve Regina graduate Ellen Roney Hughes, who reported that she was curator for a national exhibit on sports memorabilia at the Smithsonian. It turned into a more comprehensive feature on her hobby and her career, written by a student, which was in response to another feedback item submitted by a reader who said they'd like to see more stories written by students."

When the survey was first launched, the university received roughly 12 completed surveys each week. Since that time the number of responses has decreased.

"The pace has slowed, but it is understandable as the university now implements several methods for communicating with its readers to garner editorial content for the magazine," says Boxler. "Examples include the office of alumni, parents and friends' use of Harris Connect, an online community through which readers can submit their own personal news, career news, upload photos, etc. Additionally, the development office's phonathon callers ask for updated news and events that can be included in the magazine."

While they are not currently promoting the online survey, Boxler says plans are to do so in a variety of ways.

"When the survey is reworked and improved, we plan to direct readers to it via the magazine itself, the university website and by establishing links on the emerging social media electronic avenues," the public information officer says.

Sources: Matt Boxler, Public Information Officer; Deb Herz, Managing Editor of Publications; University Relations and Advancement, Salve Regina University, Newport, RI. Phone (401) 341-2156 (Boxler) or (401) 847-6650 (Herz). E-mail: boxlerm@salve.edu or herzd@salve.edu

---

Four Steps to Online Survey Success

Looking to create a reader survey? Matt Boxler, public information officer, Salve Regina University (Newport, RI), offers four tips for reader survey success:

1. Make your surveys multi-dimensional.

2. Welcome constructive criticism.

3. Offer readers incentives for participating in the survey as a means to motivate them and to get a wider cross-section.

4. Structure questions to have a balance of open-ended and close-ended responses.

 ## Website Marketing Tip

■ If you are able to determine which of your website pages or sections is viewed most frequently (your high-traffic areas), place a link to those sections on your home page, making it even easier for visitors to connect with information they seek.